RETALIATION
AT THE HIGHEST LEVEL

RETALIATION

AT THE HIGHEST LEVEL

*Why CEOs, Boards of Directors and HR
need to change the culture*

Tools Included

JUDY FOLEY

This is a true story. It includes my personal story of sex discrimination, harassment, and retaliation. It is my best recollection of the events described. Any errors or mistakes are unintentional. I have changed the names of any individuals and organization involved as it is not my purpose to cause anyone harm. Given what I have been through, this is a story of recovery and not an attempt at revenge. I hope others can learn from my experience and understand how important it is for corporations to allow everyone to bring their whole selves to the workplace every day.

Mission: To create culture change and equity in the workplace

Learning Objectives for Retaliation at the Highest Level: Why CEO's, Boards of Directors, and HR need to change the culture

- Learn from my personal story of sex discrimination, harassment and retaliation

- Eliminate and minimize sexual misconduct in the workplace

- Understand impact on individual, families, brand, stock, employees and company

- Consider views from Psychological Expert, Trauma Expert and Legal Expert

- Learn from EEOC Study and Best Practices

- Utilize lessons learned for individuals going through Discrimination, Harassment and Retaliation

- Review considerations for Forward Thinking Companies

- How each of us can contribute to the Call to Action

My husband at the time — now ex-husband, was a saint and supported me both mentally and financially while I recovered from my experience. He was there to listen when I shared what I was enduring each day at work and worked with me to strategize throughout the ordeal. My children, my ex-husband and my family were and continue to be a source of strength for me. My values and my faith in God remain unshaken. While I am Lutheran based on religious background, I visited the Catholic Church across the street from where I worked each day and prayed, I would be given the strength and direction to lead me through this. My friends have also been a source of on-going support even though I was never able to explain the complete details of what had happened to me. My family, friends, and my belief in God allowed me to survive and tell this story.

ACKNOWLEDGEMENT

- My husband and now ex-husband, has been my best friend. He supported me in every way throughout the experience, recovery and writing the book. I can never say thank you enough for his commitment and support.

- My family, extended family and friends thank you for always being there for me.

- Our friend, an expert employment lawyer, was a support to both my husband and me throughout this journey. Mere words cannot express how much we appreciated his counsel, guidance, and how much his friendship means to us.

- My friend now, an expert in Clinical Social Work and Therapist, LCSW, ACSW, thank you for your contribution to the book and first-hand personal experience.

- My friend now, an expert who is a Registered Nurse, has a Master's Degree in Counseling and Guidance, a Reiki Master and is certified in Spiritual Guidance. She is an oblate for a monastery in Madison, WI area. Thank you for sharing your expertise in trauma.

- My pastors were amazing listeners and provided prayer to move me forward. Thank you.

- My entrepreneurial friend, saw in me an entrepreneurial spirit. He asked me to initiate a collaborative organization formed with C-level executives focused on enabling established entrepreneurs to achieve breakthrough business success. This helped me develop new skills prior to returning to the work force.

- My mentor, since 2010 shared experiences, insights on his relationships, and his approach to building organizations through mergers and acquisitions, his passion. He exposed me to a world that I never would have been exposed to or participated in based upon my upbringing and work experience.

- For all the executives and managers, I met when I could not return to work based on my horrible experience. Each of you shared personal stories of overcoming issues, helping me see my skill sets in a different light while opening my mind to opportunities that I did not see at the time. Thank you ALL - This meant the world to me at the time and allowed me to initiate new career opportunities. Keep sharing your stories as they are a source of inspiration to those whom you meet.

ABOUT THE AUTHOR

- Judy Foley, founder and CEO for The Culture of Trust, which partners collaboratively with our clients to empower them to achieve exceptional business results by unleashing their organizations full potential regarding culture, leadership and strategy to achieve a diverse and inclusive organization. Also, she is the founder and CEO of Navigate Transformation, a company focused on accelerating growth and achieving competitive advantage through transformational change in supply chain, sourcing, operations, leadership and strategy.

- She is an experienced business management executive who has been successful in corporate and consulting environments – from global technology/telecommunications, consumer packaged goods (CPG), automotive, insurance/financial services, healthcare, chemical, and non-profits to private equity-funded industrial companies and privately-owned businesses. Her credentials include hands-on operational experience working with boards of directors, C-suite executives and leadership teams on strategy, leadership skills, change management, transformation, supply chain, global sourcing, mergers & acquisition integrations, process re-engineering, and operational excellence.

- Active in the community, Judy serves on a number of boards and committees. She is a mentor to college students and consults with entrepreneurs and mid-sized businesses. She worked as a board member at LaunchX, Northwestern University's summer program that taps the potential of ambitious high school students, supporting them through the process of launching startups.

She finds it exciting to help young people achieve their dreams and make our world a better place, as the youth are our future!

- Judy is proud to be co-founder and a charter member of The Bridge, a collaborative organization - formed with C-level executives from major corporations - focused on enabling established entrepreneurs to achieve business success. Judy earned her Master's in Business Administration (MBA) with concentration in Operations and Marketing from DePaul University's Charles H. Kellstadt Graduate School of Business and holds a BS in Business Administration from the University of Wisconsin – Stout. She has also completed Lean Six Sigma Green Belt Training at Chicago Deming Association, Six Sigma Master's Program. She has certifications as a Holistic Life Coach and Women's Issues and Diversity. Participated in Leadership America National and participates in Leader Women International.

- Her father was an entrepreneur and Judy's mom managed the financial statements. Her father passed away from heart failure at 49 and left four children, 17, 14, 7 and 5 years old. This was two weeks before Judy's eighth birthday. Her mom was leading-edge for her time. When she assumed her roles as widow, mother, veteran and support for the family in 1968 there were very few divorcees and single mothers. She taught her children to go after their dreams no matter what obstacles came before them.

- Judy resides in the Chicago suburbs. She is blessed to have two sons, a daughter, and an ex-husband who have supported her through tough experiences and challenges. Judy loves them all deeply.

CONTENTS

CHAPTER 1

INTRODUCTION

"Each of us is defined by our values, beliefs and upbringing.
It took courage to address sexual discrimination, harassment,
and retaliation in the workplace. It takes courage to take
back our power to tell our stories."

—JUDY FOLEY

Have you ever walked into a situation where a person is being belit-
tled or bullied in the workplace? What have you witnessed in the
workplace that was uncomfortable, reproachable, or just unacceptable? Have you stepped in, or has fear of losing your job stopped
you? Did the workplace also promote a common vision and set of
values with the goal of enhancing respect and collaboration across
the workforce?

I was a part of an organization that reflected both aspects of the
above behaviors. The company promoted the need for a respectful
work culture while tolerating disrespectful and hurtful behavior that
undermined the stated and documented common vision and values.
I loved my job and collaborated well with the people. I was a top

performer and was included in a high-performance mentor program where a senior vice president was assigned to mentor me. I was recognized with the "Gold FOCUS Award" for my results. The award included financial responsibility with profit, operational efficiency, customer service, understanding risk and underwriting excellence, and stakeholder value. I was promoted three times at this company. I had experienced growth, development, opportunities, and numerous promotions throughout my career based on my honesty, work ethic, knowledge, and teamwork at other large corporations. When I faced some uncomfortable situations with a particular executive, I set some boundaries in a one-on-one discussion, believing I could continue working with this individual. I never expected the outcome that would come from this discussion and how my world would be turned upside down. Intuitively, I started to see changes that did not feel right. My boss was now retreating from his prior comment to me, "You are going nowhere but up from here." I was guided by integrity and my belief that the right thing would occur. However, my new world was one where I was ostracized, excluded, and lacked personal and professional respect in an organization where I had dedicated so much of my energy and time. The legal term was "retaliation," but my life suffered more than I ever imagined.

My husband, an executive at a Fortune 500 firm, never believed this would happen at his company. He stated. "the behavior and tactics shown to me would have resulted in termination had they occurred in the organization, where he worked." Yet one executive I turned to for his insight, shared this occurs in most corporations because they want to protect executives key to the organization. He shared, "this was never about you, it was protecting the executive." Yet I suffered and felt the long-term effects of these actions for 8 years plus an additional 1.5 years addressing them.

What happened next for me was not about money, restitution, or finding justice. I learned that many who experience humiliation, bullying, harassment and retaliation in the workplace have very few places to go even to understand what happened to them. The legal system provides very little help if you simply want to put your life back together. Retaliation can and does lead to profound personal and professional consequences.

My purpose is to share my journey by focusing on what I learned. This experience happens every day in any organization be it a corporation, hospital, school, church, politics, etc. My experiences are relevant not just for those facing similar challenges in their organization but for the organization and its Board of Directors, CEO's, executives, human resources, and management. The cost of retaliation knows no boundaries and ultimately destroys the talent and lives of those who are witnesses and victims alike.

The "me too" or "times up" movement are just slogans unless you see the realities that are played out every day. What is in it for you? I will share what it was like for me and 10 lessons learned from my experience, I learned what happens every day in institutions where position trumps reality. This is the way it looks. We become a COG in the system. We need to learn the true realities, learn how we must change the current culture and our actions that occur because of these situations. There are tools in this book that will help Board of Directors, CEO's, HR, and corporate management change the way issues are handled to manage their company brand, eliminate bullying, retaliation and achieve better results. There are tools for employees that have been in this situation, are in this situation or prepare others with signs that this may be an issue within the corporation.

The fallout is occurring in churches such as Bill Hybels at Willow Creek Church, Roger Ailes at Fox News, Harvey Weinstein in Hollywood, and corporations where issues like these are hidden behind non-disclosures agreements where money is paid out to silence the victims. Fortune 100 companies are now including terms as condition of employment - to waive their right to sue and to agree that any employment-related claims will be pursued in one-on-one arbitration, where most proceedings are subject to confidentiality. Said another way, we prefer to keep our dirt in house without public exposure.

The following story is based on real events and the history of the author. Names and industry have been changed.

CHAPTER 2

MY PERSONAL STORY

"Any change, any loss, does not make us victims.
Others can shake you, surprise you, disappoint you,
but they can't prevent you from acting, from taking the situation
you're presented with and moving on. No matter where you are
in life, no matter what your situation, you can always do something.
You always have a choice and the choice can be power."

—Blaine Lee,
The Power Principle

This is my story. It's tough for me to share, as it is so painful. I want readers to learn what happened to me and how things unfolded, because **it could be your story**.

I was the victim of sexual discrimination, harassment, and retaliation at a large company. I shared my story with lawyers and they determined what laws were being broken and the charges. In this book, I want to share the life-changing, career-changing and personal impacts that something like this can have on you, on your family and life in general. In addition, I want to share the lessons I learned so you are more informed on this subject and will understand what to do.

Did I ever expect this? No. Did I see it coming? Not initially. If you think something is changing but you don't specifically know what to look for, you may believe you can manage through it yourself.

At the beginning of this story, actions by management happened that impacted my credibility, reputation, and undermined my career. My instincts told me something wasn't right. Other employees were making me aware of odd things occurring around me. I thought I could work through it and resolve these issues based on my past experience, the results I had achieved for the company, and my established business relationships. I was wrong. Listen to your internal compass – it's usually right.

This undermining was like a river that kept flowing and building with time. The power behind it became more damaging over time, like a flood that was out of control, flowing everywhere. When I addressed my concerns, I knew I had been given the personal strength to speak up and address issues that had benefited me throughout my career. I needed to attempt to change what was occurring to me and not allow this to happen to others.

A culture has been created over hundreds of years regarding issues of sexual discrimination, sexual harassment, harassment, retaliation, and bullying. Those who leverage this tactic remain under the radar because people are silenced from speaking their truth.

I called my husband daily to share what was occurring and what I was being taken to task on. He was surprised when I would share the details for the day and how the company was approaching this. I went daily to a church across the street from the company, prayed to God every day and left it in his hands. I said, "God if you want me to share this story then I am not to sign a non-disclosure. I leave this in your hands."

I wasn't new to this company. I had enjoyed over three years there. I was naïve; I never knew this type of action occurred in businesses. I was big on trust and my eyes were opened from this experience. In my search for books on sexual discrimination, harassment and retaliation during my journey I found zero books at Barnes and Noble or the library. I discovered and read *The Speed of Trust: The One Thing that Changes Everything* by Stephen Covey. I shared this book with one of the top executives in charge of the administration of the division. I also shared with my boss and coworkers a brief summary of the book. I invited them to read it by sharing the three copies on my desk that I would lend to anyone interested in reading. This was my way of expressing that things were not right and to stay aware. I fought what was occurring with everything I had.

I also wanted to share that, without trust, an organization cannot achieve the best results. I even placed a quote from Covey's book on my whiteboard. ***"Over time, I have come to this simple definition of leadership: Leadership is getting results in a way that inspires trust."*** But any trust I had in the company was shattered over a period of 18 months.

The Speed of Trust addresses the following: "There is one thing that is common to every individual, relationship, team, family, organization, nation, economy, and civilization throughout the world – one thing which, if removed, will destroy the most powerful government, the most successful business, the most thriving economy, the most influential leadership, the greatest friendship, the strongest character, the deepest love.

On the other hand, if developed and leveraged, that one thing has the potential to create unparalleled success and prosperity in every dimension of life. Yet, it is the least understood, most neglected, and most underestimated possibility of our time.

That one thing is ***trust***."

Before this experience, I had never been exposed to such evil in the world and predatory practices. It's interesting this experience allowed the people who initiated these actions to keep their jobs, while I suffered for "speaking the truth." I know if I turn my head and do not attempt to change this from happening to others, it will continue. The only way to change this and make a difference is by nurturing a new culture of trust and *not* allowing these circumstances to be accepted by leadership, CEO's, boards of directors and leaders in human resources. This is the change we need to see to stop these deeds from reoccurring.

It has taken me nearly 10 years to recover from this experience. My trust in companies was severely impacted by this organization and the leaders that participated in these inappropriate actions. My boss and I had a great business relationship before this, yet I learned very quickly anything can be done if it is supported by the CEO and leadership. I relived events daily for about three years. I used a variety of therapies including silent retreats, counselor's, pastor's, a trauma expert, energy experts, and reiki experts to help me. I can now use my years of recovery to help companies, boards of directors, CEOs, HR personnel, lawyers, and victims who have gone through this – or will.

MY FIRST FEW YEARS WITH THE COMPANY

When I was hired into this company in June 2005, I brought a wealth of talent, proficiency, and executive experience in operations, marketing, procurement, and insurance products management while working for other Fortune 100 companies.

During my first two years, I was a dedicated and tireless professional, working 60-hour weeks, with the right mix of leadership drive, teamwork sensitivity, and major accomplishments. I produced results. For example, I led executive relationship meetings with a strategic supplier that led to beneficial modification in the master agreement with a million dollars savings and reengineered processes with cross functional teams for multiple commodities, establishing KPI's and savings of millions of dollars for additional categories and contracts before I went to work with another part of organization. In the second quarter of my second year, I was asked to work with the vice president in that organization, as my peer with ten years of expertise, was not meeting sourcing strategy needs. When I took that position to establish strategy, I created a process which included analyzing data, prioritizing commodities based on impact, running cross functional teams to reengineer processes and establishing measurements of success. My work resulted in new ways to prioritize a variety of areas for maximum results.

I achieved three promotions in three years, with a base increase of 52% in that time. A year-end bonus alone was 23% over a base increase of 25%, and I received the highest possible rating. I had established myself as a dedicated professional who brought the right mix of leadership drive and teamwork sensitivity.

I was assigned a Senior Vice President (SVP) to me as my mentor for high potential employees. I earned an award for my financial impact, superior team dedication, and contributions towards establishing a new organization within the company while still doing my regular job which became an 80 hour week. This organization was created based on my contributions, processes, measurements and contract requirements I defined from my experience initially for Adam's area. The outcome was streamlined processes, reduced cycle time, reduced supplier count, higher expectations for suppliers that resulted in major cost savings and defined key performance indicators (KPI's). This strategy and structure were a completely new approach that the company had not previously done.

In other words, I was a model employee making significant cost savings and improvements in the operational aspects of what we did. There was no reason for me to think of the future as anything but rosy.

A NEW OPPORTUNITY: MAY 2007

At the end of May 2007, my boss, Dick, asked me to meet with Adam (not real names), the vice president of one of the company's main divisions, to introduce myself and share my approach to strategy and the sourcing process. Dick told me that my peer, who had reported to him had been supplying only reports, and Adam was frustrated because he had not addressed the strategy and plan that he was hoping for. Dick was sure I could deliver on this based on my performance on other commodities and the wins I had already established.

Before the meeting, Dick said, "This area is a man's world. Are you up for the challenge?" I said "yes" as I'd worked with men for most of my career. I shared I was capable of learning new commodities quickly. I made certain Adam knew going in I was not familiar with his area of expertise for the business, but I would quickly dig in to understand this new area of focus. Also, I had demonstrated in the past that I successfully completed strategy development and had produced outstanding results in other commodities I had worked on. My boss said, "Judy, you'll know by Friday if you are going to work with him."

I met with the VP, Adam on Wednesday to introduce myself and share my approach on strategy and sourcing process. He shared his frustrations about my peer, and how he had provided operational reports, but no go forward strategy. I listened and took in how Adam addressed his concerns. I explained my approach to establishing strategy, priorities, and my expectations that his team would be a part of a cross functional team to establish these new requirements. By setting the bar higher, we would be capable of producing better results for the organization. He was impressed with my approach and stated he enjoyed meeting me. The meeting was successful, professional and pleasant.

On Friday my boss, Dick relayed to me, "I am getting another promotion effective July 1 because the pay scale is higher in this division and that Adam, VP wants me to work with him." I get the green light to establish a strategy in June,2007, gained buy in from Adam on a plan of action, the team members needed, and the measures of success. We work through data accuracy issues, root caused them and how these actions could be addressed by his team so the data at the basis for our strategy could be corrected and provided a clear picture of his operational performance. Once we had gathered the updated data that accurately reflected his business, a final strategy was agreed upon and we moved forward based upon the priorities we mutually defined.

Adam and I worked well together, and he bought into my process approach and outcomes. I was very successful in working with the cross functional team to reengineer the processes for his specific area, establish best in class suppliers, and influence the new process with suppliers. The outcome of this work was streamlined processes, reduced cycle time, reduced suppliers to manage more easily, higher expectations with best in class suppliers while achieving major cost savings and defined KPI'S. We were quickly and methodically making a number of improvements in this group and the overall organization was very complimentary about the changes being made. We were both receiving accolades for our results.

During that same year, I also worked with the senior executives in this division on roadmaps to understand our critical supplier's needs and future plans as well as the company's strategic objectives. This allowed us to determine where changes would benefit each organization for the future and allowed all to strategically plan better. Over time, I was working on multiple larger initiatives with other organizations utilizing the same process now for other product lines. My approach was achieving success in multiple areas of the business.

SUPPLIER MANAGEMENT ORGANIZATION (STARTED JANUARY 2008)

In January 2008, in further recognition of my strong performance, I was promoted to the position of Director of Procurement in the divisions Sourcing area. In this role, my key assignment was to serve as an internal consultant for the division, working for Dick my boss, charged with conceptualizing and delivering a "best in class "Centralized Supplier Management Organization. As part of this effort, I worked with Adam and his team in this division.

I accomplished a great deal for this division and my process was the basis for the Supplier Management Organization being developed to achieve these benefits and learn from my implementations corporate wide. Established standard work procedures that highlighted lessons learned, an approach to process improvement, and detailed plans that would work effectively for this new supplier management organization. I used my experience of implementing a global system and process at a previous employer for consideration when the two project planners and I sat down to establish the initial project plan for the new organization. My experiences there helped to mitigate a number of stumbling blocks that the planners had not envisioned at the time we had met. I was also instrumental in overseeing the three phases of project/organization/implementation based on my experience with this division and created the standardized scorecard for use with our suppliers. I was a key member in defining the job descriptions for the new organization, but was later surprised when Dick, my boss, shared that sourcing details, a cornerstone of the organizational design, was being removed from the job description.

PORTENTS OF THINGS TO COME: APRIL 2008

> "I am a person that looks at everything with a half full glass
> verses a half empty glass. I give people the benefit of the doubt."

Things continue to work well with Adam and the organization over the next twelve months. In April, he invited me to join him at a conference to learn about his area of the business. He meets me every morning at my shuttle for the conference and mentors me about specific expertise and categories for his area of the business and the industry. I came to this conference with the intention to learn as much as I could about these areas and it had further improved my understanding of a close network of suppliers and those, they did business with. A couple of days into the conference, as we were reviewing exhibits together, we met a supplier representative who invited Adam for cocktails to discuss business and, in turn, Adam invited me. I was excited and proud that he was bringing me along as a peer. Based on the discussion with the representative Adam suggested that we take a trip to visit and understand their supplier's contractor program together based on the conversation with the representative. My first indication of things to come was while we were talking about business; I noticed Adam kept looking at my legs throughout the discussion.

Also, while we were reviewing exhibits, he shared with me how his brother-in-law wanted a divorce from his sister. The brother-in-law was working to get everything in the divorce. He shared he hired a company he had used for work to get the details on his brother-in-law. He said I fixed that and his sister received everything in her favor. I remember thinking, I don't want to mess with him based on how he handled this.

On another day, during one of the conference classes, Adam paged me six times. When I finally stepped into the hall to find out what he needed, he told me his meeting had ended early; could we meet sooner than we had originally planned to? I agreed, yet I was surprised that he needed to be so persistent about the follow up. At other times — he said things like, "I really need someone like you," that made me question why he was saying this. At one point, he asked about my kids' ages. When he found out they weren't young, he said, "Oh, good – I'm glad your kids are older." I remember feeling somehow that he was inferring a further relationship, and my not having young kids would be a benefit.

At this conference, I helped Adam plan a dinner for some of his staff as he had not scheduled it and it was the next evening. I am an organized person, so I offered to work out the details – the restaurant, the menu, and coverage for attendees. Attendees are mainly men with only two other women attending the dinner. At first, I planned to sit next to him, but since so many new people were present, I suggested that he get to know some of his new employees that he had not met, so I sat at the far end of the table allowing him to get to know others and me to meet new people within his team. Adam made a couple of odd statements to me from the other end of the table, such as, "Judy what did you order for dinner? "I stated "turkey." He states "I love turkey and almost ordered the same but instead ordered fish since we were in Boston." A few minutes later he stated "Judy, did I tell you my wife is of Spanish descent?" What did *that* mean? I was not sure of the significance, but I let it go and felt other people thought this was an unusual statement as did I.

Things continued to happen after we returned back at the office. A series of comments in multiple settings began to a resurface on a more frequent basis.

- At a meeting with one of Adam's direct reports, Adam said out of the blue, "Judy, should start traveling with us." direct reports reaction was "no." I was surprised by the suggestion. I knew my boss would never agree to that as I had other responsibilities beyond the work I was supporting for Adam's team.

- One morning right after a conference at work, Adam said, "You're going to want to be with me every day." I didn't respond as was surprised by the comment, but I thought, "If he says that again, I'll need to resolve this."

- I noticed that Adam seemed to keep the same hours as I. No matter when I sent an email, even on weekend mornings or late evenings, he responded immediately.

- Another time he states you must have been a Girl Scout based on your organizational skills and the fact you are always prepared for meetings. I did not respond to this statement and moved on to the agenda at hand.

- Another time I come into the office dressed in a hot pink dress. He states I do not believe I have ever had anyone in my office in all pink before. I did not reply and moved on to the agenda at hand.

- When I returned from a cruise with my family, Adam told me how wonderful and tan I looked. He told me how much he wanted to go on a cruise – just like me. He often brought up things we seemed to have in common. At the time, I suggested my sister's family had taken her children when they were younger on a Walt Disney Cruise and that he and his family might enjoy this as an option.

- After a vacation at my brother's cottage, I told him about riding a jet ski at 60 miles per hour and how exhilarating it was. Now, at the conference in Boston, he had told me "he wasn't into athletic stuff." After his vacation the very next week after mine, he brought it up – in a business conversation – how *he* loved to Jet Ski at 60 miles per hour. He stated "you seem surprised by this" as now I have paused the conversation as I am a bit thrown off by the comment. I stated "I didn't know you jet ski" and he states "oh yes."

- I went on a vacation with friends and family camping. He asks about my vacation and I share how enjoyable it was. He shares he is thinking about buying lake property and placing a camper on it. It appears he is trying to show me where we have similarities.

- One day, he asked me to call him at a certain time in the morning when he was working at home. He answered the phone, saying," I just stepped out of the shower and am drying myself off." I thought it was odd he was not prepared for the meeting and a strange and inappropriate thing to say to me. I focused on the agenda at hand and he said he would call me back to address the issues we had planned to review.

PROMOTIONAL OPPORTUNITY JUNE AND JULY 2008

In June, Dick, my boss called me to say he has seen the potential structure for a new organization of the business, and an assistant vice president position would be open. He said I'd have a good chance of getting it based on my skill sets, qualifications and achievements in the organization and his specific area of expertise.

Both Adam and Dick, my boss had told me I was the most qualified for this role in two separate meetings. I met Adam for lunch during the first week of July. Adam had stated that I should "own the position and make it my own based on what I had accomplished to date, and that we would make an excellent team." "Dick had told me that although two people were being considered for the job, I was the most prepared for the position and, based on my results, I would get it." Dick stated, "the other person under consideration was an IT Supplier Manager with no experience in Adam's expertise area or the division." He went through a list of people who would not be considered. He mentioned there was someone who was studying to be a lawyer but she did not have enough experience in the division to be considered. The prior manager whom I had replaced, who does not get the respect from this division and his past performance would eliminate him from consideration. The other leaders whose lack of experience in this area would eliminate them from consideration.

Also, Adam had stated over our celebration of accomplishment in September given what we had accomplished together, we would be an excellent team. He had shared he was receiving accolades as well. Dick had stated confirmation along the way as well.

THE CELEBRATION OF ACCOMPLISHMENT WITH VP, ADAM – AUGUST 2008

Preface to this meeting: A day we are both working from home in the middle of my sentence, I hear Adam add something into the discussion which I did not fully understand I stated can you repeat that? He states, "I think we should go out for a celebratory drink now that the project is complete and we've accomplished so much. I said "that would be nice" and moved on to the business at hand. We agree on a time later and he picks the location.

NOTE to readers: I will tell this story in the present tense, as it makes the story more real. I can remember this day like it was yesterday. It is etched in my memory forever.

On the day of the celebration of accomplishments – the Friday before Labor Day – I run into Adam in the hallway near his office. He is actually shimmying his shoulders at me, which I find not just unprofessional but a bit odd. Another associate, comes around the corner at the same time and I gave Adam a look of disdain. He stops and asks him, "have you met Judy Foley." associate states, "I do not believe so." I stated "yes, we worked on the salvage RFP with my direct report." "Oh yes" now he recalls.

Adam asks me to meet him in the lobby of our building. I arrive before he does, so I text to ask when he'll be ready. He says he's in a strategy meeting that's running late. When he shows up, he seems very happy to see me, and I am looking forward to learning more about his meeting and him. He escorts me to a nearby and rather outdated lounge not at all what I am accustomed to, where we sit at the bar.

We order drinks and appetizers, and he toasts me – and us – for our accomplishments. We agree that we work well together, shown by our great results. He says something odd – that he "could say anything he wanted about this night." When I mentioned I hope not, I have a good reputation to keep" he states "I'm just joking."

I order a cosmopolitan martini. Adam calls me a "lush" for ordering such a drink. I reply, "No one has ever called me a lush, and I'm not sure I want to stay when you call me a lush!" Again, he says, "I'm just joking."

At this point, I consider leaving, as this opening conversation feels inappropriate. But as we start talking about business, I feel more comfortable as he seems more like the person I know. We spend quite a bit of time talking about that day's strategy meeting, where the division is going in the future, my future role in the organization, his role, and what we will accomplish together moving forward. Also, we talk about the Supplier Management Organization and the direction the organization needs to take in order to be effective along with a consistent information technology (IT) plan.

After about a half-hour, Adam gets a call from his office – he left some confidential information on a credenza. He excuses himself to take care of the problem, leaving me alone for about 20 minutes.

Adam returns, sweating and a bit out of breath from his running. He notices that (of course) some of my drink is gone. He asks, "Did you order another drink while I was gone? You lush." I replied" no it's the same drink." Two things occur to me- first, he seems cheap and concerned about the cost of the drink; second, what kind of a man calls a woman a "lush" and is so disrespectful? Throughout the night, I never finished my second drink while Adam consumed 2 martinis and 2 beers. I remember questioning if he should be mixing drinks but he responded this was best for him.

Adam walks over to the jukebox and selects some songs. He plays "Hey, Jude" and mouths the words to the song to me. He is being very flirtatious and suggests that I select more songs. We do this together.

Back at the bar, the bartender asks Adam if he wants to watch the football game. Adam says that he is "directed completely at this beautiful lady, not football." He tells me about a woman lawyer whom he was involved with from his last job who followed him from St. Louis to Chicago. He said he didn't plan to marry her and wanted nothing to do with her now. I know Adam is married, so I am surprised he is sharing this with me. To make things worse, he asks me what I would do in her situation. This seems so inappropriate, but I say that if I were her and single, I wouldn't have wasted my time – I would have dated someone else.

We move on to talk about work projects, travel we have done and other things related to our jobs. His phone rings – it's his wife. I can hear the whole conversation. He tells her he's in a meeting with other executives and is short and to the point with her. I hear her ask if he'd be home in time to see their boys, and he says he'll try.

Now, he turns the conversation to his wife. Before they had a family, he says, they would "go out for appetizers and drinks before kids." In retrospect, I see it is similar to what we were doing. He shares he asks her to accompany him to events, instead she declines his request and stays home with the kids. His wife has never hired a babysitter for the kids. He shared that he and his wife have a good relationship, but she's a stay-at-home mom who doesn't relate to his work. He says they don't go out to eat because she doesn't trust restaurants based on her experience and what she knows occurs in kitchens. He states how he loves to eat multiple-course meals – in direct conflict with what he stated at the Conference. He also comments he appreciates my expertise and the knowledge of the workplace. I listen as it seems he needs a sounding board.

Adam shares he has not seen his kids over the last few days. I ask about his kids and if he has been out like this the last couple of nights? He is surprised by my question. He says no, that when he arrived home the kids were playing with friends and only came back in time to go to bed.

Adam shares more about his personal life. He has a sweet tooth but lost 19 pounds over the last couple of months. He rides his bike with his kids to the next town for sundaes. I shared that when my husband and I were in college we would run every night, and then afterwards get ice cream near our dorm. These will be special memories his children will cherish. He shares he doesn't speak Italian, even though it's his ethnic language as his father wanted them to fit in and just speak English. His father worked at a company climbing poles to fix issues for electric company and his mom did not work. He and his dad know how to connect the dots about stocks and talk daily. I get the impression that while he is talking, he thinks less of his mother than his father. Then he asks about what my parents did. I tell him that my father owned his own business, he passed away when I was young, and my mom was his bookkeeper. He asks how old I was? My dad died just two weeks before my eighth birthday. I shared I can remember his death and every detail like it was yesterday and it was the worst thing that ever happened to me. I say that I could live through anything as I lived through that. (I did not know what experience was to come and how those words would be tested.) I tell him that my mother did well raising four children on her own at a time when there were few divorces and I did not know of any widows among my classmates in 1968. I share that my sister and I became strong women based on losing our father and the fact my mom was such a strong woman managing issues that most women did not handle at that time. Twice during my story, he says, "Just what we need – more really strong women." When I ask him why, he says that men in general don't like strong women, and we must deal with that enough in the workplace. I feel that I'm I seeing a new aspect of this man.

My older son calls to ask when I'd be home, and I say I'll be leaving on the 7:30 train. Adam asks if I told him where I was. When I say no, he says, "You didn't tell him you were a lush and out drinking?" Then he adds, "Just kidding." I am amazed he is even saying this to me. I thought at the time, my husband knows where I am but your wife has no idea based on his phone call.

When Adam asks about my husband, I share information about the roles he has had in his career, where he works and how smart he is. Adam asks if my husband makes me laugh? I say yes, he has a good sense of humor and makes me laugh. I thought this question was odd and wondered why he would ask it.

At least twice, Adam says, "Next time, we should start our time together at 2 pm." He insinuates that this could become a regular thing, shared that we could leave early from work and that it would be okay. I say that my boss would never let me leave work early, and this would never be acceptable. We talked about staying until the 8:30 train. He asks, how long I could be out before my husband would question me? I say that my husband has always trusted me and there would be no reason to question me. He is surprised by response. At 7:10, I say that I am leaving to catch my train. He walks me out to the taxi, and the evening is over. On my way home on the train I am upset, I write down everything we talked about including the strange statements Adam made.

My husband is away for the weekend for an annual motorcycle ride with my brothers and brother-in-law. I plan to meet my sister for dinner the next night. I tell her everything, sharing the notes I took. She states I handled myself well and did all the right things. I say that I'll tell my husband about this when he gets home as I have always been 100% honest with him. But my sister says there's no need to do that, as I had handled the situation. I did not know at the time that she had never been exposed to how this is handled in the business world as she is in the medical field. At the time, she had no idea– nor did I – how this night would impact my life, as well as my husband's and our family's. That night, we innocently believed this situation was resolved.

ESTABLISHING BOUNDARIES WITH VP. ADAM – SEPTEMBER 2008

By Sunday night I have thought about it so much, I decided to speak with Adam when we returned to work on Tuesday. I wanted to be sure that he understood that I could not be involved in a "personal relationship." Tuesday morning, I called him and said that I needed to talk with him for the last time. He asked, "The last time?" I said yes. He told me to come up right then – at 6:30 am.

Before I went to his office, I reviewed the notes I had established for the meeting. I started to go up twice and turned around twice. When I entered his office, Adam said something odd – that he might not "sound like himself" because he'd just read an article about a "jungle at the zoo." I believed he might sound different because he was uneasy and stressed about what I was about to discuss.

He said that he could see that I was visibly upset. My approach was controlled and not confrontational. When I started to talk, he became extremely nervous. I mentioned that we had an "amazing chemistry together" – by which I meant that we worked really well together. As I tried to read my notes, the words were a blur, so I did this by memory. I shared with Adam that I had spoken to my sister about my feelings and concerns. I said I'd put myself out on a limb. I meant when I went with him alone to celebrate our work, and I had never done this before. I had trusted him, and believed I would be okay. I said that I had been married for 24 years and had always been faithful and never cheated on him. I told him that I could never be "number two" in his life. Twice, he asked, "What do you mean, you put yourself out on a limb?" I heard him, but kept going while I still had the courage and determination. I never answered him.

When I was finished, he said that he'd been married for 12 years plus 2 years, 14 years and had never cheated. He asked, "Where did you get this from?" I believed he was referring to my clarification about what was said during our celebration of accomplishment, and I was addressing my concerns that this could never be. He knew as well as I where I "got this from," and how he had alluded that our meeting could become a regular thing at 2 pm – and told me about the lawyer who he was involved with and had followed him to Chicago from his last job.

Adam leaned back in his chair and said, "It's a normal thing to go out for drinks." He said he was sorry if he had said anything to lead me to this conclusion. My reply was "Okay, fine," and I left. I knew he was protecting himself. But he understood where I stood, and that was what I had wanted from the meeting.

When I got back to my desk, I called Adam and discussed "some upcoming projects and stated my next steps, to show we could work together." At this point, I believed that I had established that we could work together and had just set appropriate boundaries. I had no intention to get him in trouble. I wasn't planning to take this to Human Resources, since we were two professionals and we could move on. I didn't know it at the time, but this was the beginning of a long, painful episode in my life. I had thought the death of my father was the worst thing that had happened in my life, yet this was far worse.

ADAM'S ACTIONS CHANGE AND OPPORTUNITY GONE – SEPTEMBER TO DECEMBER 2008

Following that conversation with Adam on that Tuesday after Labor Day 2008 where I communicated my objections, a series of actions marked an abrupt, negative change in how he treated of me – and this was only the beginning of what was to come.

Before the night at the bar, Adam had trusted me and had complete confidence in the work I was doing. He had had complete belief and was confident that I could cover the needs of his organization. After I addressed my concerns and rejected any further relationship except business, he took on stronger coordination of projects with his team by himself, and new initiatives did not come to me. His approach with me changed. He basically isolated me, excluded me from meetings, communications, and initiatives. This negatively impacted my work and reputation as an emerging leader in the company.

During our next business meeting, Adam looked out the window rather than at me. I was part of the conversation, but anyone who knew how we usually worked together could notice a difference.

In another meeting with an outside consultant and project manager, Adam and I needed to sit next to each other to answer questions about the work I had completed for his organization gain both of our perspectives. I heard this noise, and realized that he was so nervous that he had taken off his shoes and was rubbing his feet on his shoes. He had never done this in any of my meetings in the past.

At a conference call in Adam's office with his team, we were talking about a contract, and I must have given Adam a look. He said to everyone on the phone, "Judy is mad at me." To me, this sounded like a girlfriend/boyfriend comment. After the meeting, I provided feedback on the software contract, clarified details, and shared how this should be handled in the future. His direct report paid close attention to see how Adam was taking this feedback. (This is the same guy that I will share later said I was on probation.)

The representative we had a business conversation with at the conference reached out after this conference to say the company was having a conference and Adam stated he needed to be at a board meeting at the same time. I suggested I could go on my own and coincidentally, he added we would talk about this in the office. I documented our discussion to him in an email and was comfortable that I could attend on my own. I was eventually told no; I would not need to attend the meeting.

As time went by, I tried to act like nothing had happened, as we were two professionals. I was still doing an exemplary job in my role at the company. In fact, another executive who had worked with me on multiple projects said, "You're such a star." Looking back, I see that I was a bit naïve and assumed that all was going well – but that changed quickly when this same person told me that I had not been included in some major communications related to the work I was performing. He was perplexed as was I.

From September through the rest of 2008, my instincts told me that things were not right. In October, I talked things over with my husband and he reminded me about what my boss said at the dinner party in the summer we attended, "I was going nowhere but up from here in my career."

The dinner party was at my boss's summer house which included me, my husband, his wife, my boss and his daughter seeing a light show on the river, going on their pontoon boat and going to a restaurant for dinner. My husband thought I was misreading the situation based on my boss's statement over dinner, so initially I overrode my feelings.

By December, I realized that I was not being considered for the assistant vice president position that Adam and my boss had once told me I was most qualified for. I am made aware by my peer, Claudia who is not qualified has been selected for a director position. My peer appears to be rubbing it in my face, the fact that I am not informed and did not get the position.

At this same time Dick, my boss, is telling internal customers and executives I would no longer be working with them. My job is changing. In regards to suppliers he was telling old suppliers I would be working with them. The suppliers, clients and executives were telling me this. I acted like I knew, but was completely caught off guard. I found it interesting that I was not informed by my boss about this.

In July 2008, both Adam and my boss had told me I was the most qualified for that role in two separate meetings. Adam had stated that I should "own the position and make it your own mark based on what I had accomplished to date, and that we would make an excellent team." Dick had told me that although two people were being considered for the job, "I was the most prepared for the position and, based on my results, I would get it."

But subtle things were occurring internally. Over time, Adam began orchestrating things more overtly. People in his area of the company were asking me why I was not in meetings, and what had changed. Sadly, I saw no advocate for me – not even my own boss.

During these months, I struggled to concentrate on my work. It took more time to get the easiest things done. My boss, Dick, noticed that something was off, but I believed I was working on the problem with Adam, and I didn't want to get him into trouble or ruin his career. I remembered when my boss had told me "this area was a man's world" and I felt I could handle anything. I believed I needed to keep working through this.

Before the incident, Adam always answered my emails immediately. Now it took hours and even days. He began declining and cancelling meetings with me, and this isolated me from the team and its initiatives. I backed off on scheduling meetings and started working on other projects.

Then, Adam suddenly began criticizing my work on other initiatives and accused me of sending "too many emails." Before the incident, an IT Supplier Manager told me that I "could do no wrong – Adam loves everything about you." Now that manager told me that Adam was telling people that I was "calling him too much." I remember thinking how strange this was as I was handling meetings as I had always done. When I asked Adam about it, he said "the man had taken his words out of context." Highly doubtful!

At the point of the first big catastrophe, Adam told me quite loudly on the phone to quit sending him so many emails. In fact, he told me not to send him emails for two weeks. It seemed like he might have wanted someone else to hear him say this. So, I backed off. I completely "followed orders," as I felt he was irritated by the circumstances, and I was getting the brunt of it. I let my boss know how Adam had attacked me on two issues, but Dick gave Adam the benefit of the doubt.

This adverse shift in the way Adam treated me – which stood in such sharp contrast to his prior behavior – did not escape the notice of others on the team. One director expressed surprise that I was being left out of several critical communications. A consultant who reported directly to Adam observed that I was suddenly "put on probation." I was also being told things were being said about me and I am hearing them from the organization's people and procurement. Several of Adam's team members asked why I was not included in meetings that I usually attended. When I asked about attending other meetings, Adam told me I didn't need to attend.

BEGINNING OF OUR FRIEND, LAWYER PARTICIPATION—DECEMBER 2008

In December 2008, I shared with my husband what was occurring, what had happened and how I was no longer being considered for the AVP role I had been working towards. He thought we should talk to our friend, a global employment lawyer, so we had a phone call to share an overview. A terrible snow storm was occurring but my husband did not believe this could wait and said you need to tell him everything. Our friend and I met at a restaurant where we ordered food but I never ate a thing. When I had shared everything and explained what occurred, He said, "You know, Adam switched this all around on you from the minute you came to see him and he saw that you weren't interested in taking this further." I put my head on the table and sobbed. He suggested I pull myself together by the time he came back from the restroom. My friend gave me his insights about what was most likely occurring behind the scenes. Later I would find out his insights were right on.

After this meeting, my husband and I met daily for a month and then weekly with our friend, the employment lawyer to strategize. He shared when we went to weekly meetings if any issue came up different than our plan, he would make himself available to us no matter where he was located globally.

LOST OPPORTUNITY FOR ADVANCEMENT QUESTIONED – JANUARY–AUGUST 2009

Adam's adverse treatment of me and his dramatic withdrawal of his prior support had a larger negative impact on my work at the company. Even though leadership had previously described me as the best person for the job, I was now told that things had changed – the leadership role promised me had already been filled. Also, it was a director's role and not an AVP role.

Initially this new person, was going to go in to work with Adam and I was to prepare her for my current role. She was so nervous as she did not know how to source and did not have the skills. In the end they hired another gentleman on the outside to cover this position and she was elevated to take the leadership role that was to be my next step. Also, the Supplier Manager who is helping the Supplier Management Organization with interviewing, stated that when he interviewed her, he felt it was a stretch to make this person the - leader for this function. She had some experience in Workers Compensation, but her skills would be severely stretched with this position. He was even more surprised that the VP planned to have her run the Supplier Management Organization. She has never run a project and she had mainly handled administrative tasks in the past. Also, he was not sure with my skill set, why I was being taken off of the Supplier Management Initiative when I had contributed so much. He is surprised Dick is making this change. He states that group still respects you and your knowledge.

When I had written the job descriptions for the new organization it had certain requirements in it and Dick let me know later the sourcing requirements had been removed. Interesting how it all works together. My shock and disappointment were further compounded by what was now being asked of me to train her. Not only that, but my own boss was her official mentor. It was clear that she didn't have my skills, knowledge, and expertise, so I was suppose to help her understand what was completed or underway along with the processes I had established. I was stunned! Legally, they told me, she was qualified for the position. My legal team questioned her skill set in August.

Now, it would have been procedurally correct that Human Resources needed to post the position and put her through the interview process, but how was that accomplished after the fact that her role had already been announced informally! I was told one set of dates for the requisition and later the same day I was updated with a different date for when the requisition was posted by. I was told by my peer that the position was filled and he shared with me in December the update. Now the hiring manager, informs me the offer occurred January 6. None of the dates align properly. HR told me that everything was done per policy after their "review of what had occurred." Yet inconsistency in dates and a final update was provided to me after my letter went to the CEO in May based on my questioning!

My employment situation deteriorated further when I dared to address not being considered for that role. My boss did not appreciate my questioning of the situation. Later, he interrogated me about who I had spoken to in HR, what I said, and why I was meeting with HR. Over time, my boss pressured me to write a letter about whether I would apply for a job that was already filled and announced. I asked "why should I apply for a job that is already filled?" I documented my concerns in the letter which he did not like. It was clear that he was covering his backside to make sure he had a letter stating why I did not apply. In retrospect, it would appear that this was done primarily to close the loop on a done deal. There were two other opportunities in the organization for director positions that I was told about much later from the December announcement but they were not good choices for me given my expertise.

After my complaint, Dick now required me to submit to a 360° performance review that, in my opinion and the lawyer's opinion, was designed to solicit an unfavorable assessment. In an effort to skew the results, leadership refused to approve the raters I'd suggested – people with whom I'd worked most closely. Instead, they selected raters who aligned with Adam and Dick who didn't know me as well. HR ignored the issue. The results showed that my *clients* gave me extremely positive feedback and – not surprisingly – the skewed *peer* feedback was more negative. Also, besides the 360º review, my boss conducted one-on-one interviews with numerous people to solicit negative feedback.

I found the 360-review interesting as when I first came in, I wanted to do this the first year as an HR friend at the company had suggested this. When I suggested this to Dick, my boss, he said that I was an outstanding performer, and this was used for "problem people". So, I've gone from a star to "problem people" in a very short period of time.

I started questioning people whom my boss said were having problems or issues with me. Interestingly, his stories and theirs were different. When I shared the story, he would drop the conversation and move on to the next point. Shortly after this, he and the internal employment lawyer took away my capability to reach out to people on issues, saying only he could talk to them.

At the same time as management was undermining my performance rating, my role became more limited. The isolation and constant monitoring kept escalating, sending me a strong message that I was no longer welcome or "a star" at the company. I went from "hero to zero" over a few months.

Also, my peer had now become the golden boy in late January 2009. If you recall I was asked to work with Adam as this individual was having difficulty putting together a strategy and he was removed from the account. I had been working with him to overcome how he presented information and shared examples of presentations, strategy sessions, data and even emails. I can see the tide is changing.

RECOGNITION FEBRUARY 2009

In February of 2009, I was awarded a Gold Award for my financial impact dedication, superior team dedication, drive for success, and contributions to the Supplier Management Organization. The below comments were related directly to the award provided to me.

1 "Judy was instrumental in work to define a structure for a Centralized Supplier Management Organization, a special department will ensure proper supplier management and sustain the savings we have identified to date."

2 "Judy was a key member of this team. She worked significant hours - well beyond her expected 'day job' to provide this team with direction and focus to function." (I worked 70-80 hrs. a week during this time)

3 "I cannot say enough about the time, effort, and thought Judy has given to the project, making all of these things a reality."

The gentleman that submitted this award for approval within the company sent me an email on 2/13/2009:

Hi Judy. Congratulations! I wanted to make sure you were recognized for all of your hard work on this project, so I submitted this award on the team's behalf. Your hard work did not go without notice and appreciation. Thanks again for everything. Looking forward to continued collaboration in the future.

I received many congratulatory notes from other divisions people and peers in my organization, thanking me for the projects I had been involved in helping this organization. Even my boss is congratulating me for this award.

Interesting how my boss, Dick would not recall the collaboration it took to achieve the results for the Supplier Management Organization. He did everything in his power to show me as being a different individual.

PERFORMANCE REVIEW – FEBRUARY, MARCH, & NOW APRIL 2009

In February we talk through the review where I am told I have received the top score on my review. On March 10, Dick, my boss and I have closed the review with my score of #1 the best score you can achieve. Dick readdresses the review in March after it is closed. I was listening intently to what my boss was saying. He wrote down what little I said. Among his key points were that I was "over-interested" in a promotion when I should rectify my current role. Then he added that I should feel very good about being a #1 performer, the highest possible review score. I said, "I should, based on what I accomplished this past year, but I *don't* feel good about it. The question you should be asking is *why* I don't feel good about it." He is documenting me behind the scenes while telling me I have a number 1 rating (best achievement.) The review is closed in March again.

In April, I come back from vacation and my boss is concerned about the statement I have placed in my review response about the career position that I am not being considered for. I assumed that HR has addressed this with him and he wants me to change it. I did not change it.

The whole time, I was thinking about the documentation that just took place and how ironic this was. I had a score of #1 (the top score allowed), but my boss was documenting negative items about my performance that he could not substantiate. The two didn't jive. When I asked him to add my key accomplishments to my review, he said he couldn't do that because HR had already received it. He said he'd "think about" modifying some of the points I objected to.

MEETING WITH DICK THAT OPENS UP PERFORMANCE REVIEW – APRIL 9. 2009

The day I got back from vacation, Dick scheduled two meetings with me. I asked about issues that had arisen while I was gone. He said that peer had questions on an RFI, and I reminded him that I had told him to call me with any questions (which he hadn't done). Dick agreed and said he would talk with him.

We also talked about my annual review again, which had been reviewed in February, closed March 10, reopened in March, and now addressed in April; I had received an overall score of 1, top score. However, Dick had continued to make changes to the document through April. At this meeting, he told me he was fine with the comments I had made – except the one about the AVP position as noted below, I had been slated for and not received. At that time, I had been told I was "more than prepared for the position."

From My Review: Dick spoke with me about the draft Supplier Management Organization structure which included an AVP position supporting the team. In that discussion, I was encouraged at that time to consider myself for that AVP since I was told I was more than prepared for the position. The only significant challenge since that time was the voicing of my disappointment with Dick over the handling of the Supplier Management Organization leadership role posting and the process by which it was managed. If this issue has caused hard feelings or resentment between the two groups or has somehow diminished the view of my capabilities, that was not the intent. The intent was to clarify why I was told the position was filled prior to being given the opportunity to apply for it given my background in helping develop the Supplier Management Organization along with the prior discussions that indicated this was a good opportunity for me to consider. I still believe they were fair questions to ask. Other than this point of contention, I see no other dialog or events that point to this reduced perception in my abilities.

Dick's reply was a stunner. He said that he would have suggested that *anyone* apply for the position whether they were prepared or not! This was in direct conflict with what he has been telling me all along.

He asked if we could work through this, and I said yes. He said he was willing to work with me, but said he thought I was playing games –I stated I do not play games. He has known me since 2005 and I have always been ethical, honest, maintain high integrity and speak the truth. He knew that I had always been straightforward in my approach. I said I felt like all hell was breaking loose because I questioned how the position was handled. Nonetheless, I thought about trusting him again based on the wonderful relationship we had in the past.

Next meeting that same day I knew I could not trust him as we were going over the same points again. During this meeting, I said" you told me that I couldn't win. What did you mean by this?" He talked about the AVP position and my comments in the review again. He continued, "did I want to go over my review again?" He told me I was playing games with him. At this point, I kept the conversation to a minimum as nothing has changed and he could not be trusted.

Not long after this on May 5, I was notified that I would no longer be attending the division's Strategic meeting that required travel and my travel was cancelled at cost to the company. (No one else was dropped.) A senior vice president called to tell me that "the agenda had been changed" and the executive vice president was going to present my information. I had not been told I was going to present. My understanding was I was to listen and understand the feedback from our agents on a project I had worked on with the team. Another meeting I was to attend was also "cancelled." The messages of "no future career" continued, as did the heavy-handedness by management.

INSUBORDINATION PER BOSS AND HIGHLY SUSPECT BEING #1 EMPLOYEE < 60 DAYS 4/16/2009

In April, my boss sent a note requesting he be copied on all communication to Claudia and her direct report that worked with Adam. As noted, this morning, there has been a direct disconnect between you and this team. Also, you are to discontinue all further personal printing on Company devices. Our friend, the employment lawyer "wants this raised to HR and my mentor. It is clear he is pushing you very hard here and you have nothing to lose at this point."

Also, Dick, my boss begins sending me very obnoxious emails to me. His role reports into the Executive VP and Chief Administrative Officer for HR. He starts stating my behaviors have approached insubordination and continued behavior in this manner will lead to a Performance Plan as a next step. Every point he has I can address in a sound and reasonable manner. A Performance Plan does not occur.

My mentor, a Senior Vice President early into the high potential mentor program states, "Amazing! This is highly suspect given the #1 performance rating from 60 days ago. He suggested that it was time to involve Human Resources or a representative from the Mentor program." He cannot believe that the VP is managing personal printing. Doesn't he have bigger and better things to be worry about?" When he saw the insubordination letter, he stated "you need to get HR involved." I shared my boss reported to the Executive VP and Chief Administrative Officer for HR and I did not believe he would be objective. He suggested I speak with the mentor representative. In the end my mentor wanted to know the page that contained a funny joke for which I was reprimanded when I printed for personal printing. I shared it with him, and he laughed and said" I'd better not send it to him as he might get me fired by my boss or worse have Dick, managing his personal printing." My mentor was in full agreement that I send a letter to the CEO and stated "he would support me if he received a call from the CEO." By June, my mentor completely backed off and was no longer in contact with me. I can only assume that someone has spoken to him.

STRATEGY PLANNING WITH FRIEND, ATTORNEY – APRIL 2009

By April, I felt that everything was getting twisted, but I knew I had done the right thing by addressing this issue. Still, it remained evident my boss was putting his own spin on this.

- Our friend, the global employment lawyer, let us know the underlying issue was the protection of the VP, Adam and these other issues stem from that. My husband decided it was time to plan strategy. He wrote a letter to our friend, the lawyer, whom we had consulted from the start.

- My husband can't believe the emails going on. Hell, even the person from the mentor program does not want an email sent to him directly- this must be like watching the movie "The Departed" everyday there. I would like your thoughts on approach and probability of success for what I've drawn up below. He writes our friend, the employment lawyer per below:

THE SITUATION

- Assumption: Judy's boss's actions demonstrate he no longer wants her as a part of his team. We assume the issue over the hiring process has somehow damaged him, and he will not tolerate non-compliance to his wishes.

- She has been moved from "hero to zero." We have a good employee that is now under constant surveillance. We have a person that was recognized in 2009 for her 2008 achievements: We have a person that in 2008 received the highest performance rating you can get and has received the "gold" award for exemplary work, leadership on the Supplier Management Organization, and cost savings. An underlying fact is that she is in the high potential mentor program that is a nominated role for high performers. Time is working against us.

- The recent accomplishment works well for us now, but the longer the documentation attack continues those positive off-sets will begin to lose merit. If this persists, the documentation side of the equation will largely reduce the good base we have developed, and we'll lose its value in the discussion.

- To date, we have taken a passive counter-approach as a means of showing good faith in trying to define common ground. In contrast, his sharpness and the tone of his emails appear to be increasing in intensity indicating to me that he feels comfortable in pursuing this path without ramifications. He will, if you will, run her over and appears to show no signs of concern of rebuttal for his actions.

- Understood: We know the underlying issues are the protection of the VP, Adam and these other issues stem from that. The only logical answer given the events that have transpired can be associated with the case that centers on the outcome and frustration around the position she wanted to apply for. Once that blew up, her boss's intensity has steadily increased to a point where I could state that this has become a retaliatory event and is creating a hostile work environment and further subjecting her to harassing behavior.

- In my time in the corporate world, I have never seen emails with this much power embedded in them nor the level of scrutiny undertaken. Judy will not win this battle-the question is not if she will be let go but when…

MY GOAL (MY COMMENT AFTER THE LETTER WAS WRITTEN AND RESPONDED TO)

- Initially it was for the company to do the right thing. Either place me in another department where I could be successful or provide me some level of severance to give me time to search for a new opportunity. I always believed the right thing would be done until I could see at the end this was not going to happen.

MY GOAL NOW

- To end with the reasonable severance with the smallest amount of time investment.

SUGGESTED STRATEGY

- The current passive strategy is not working and will minimize the goal down to unemployment. I am recommending a "judo" type strategy, where we take his leads and work against him rather than continue to take the punch. A logical person (outside of company) cannot reasonably understand the zero to hero phenomenon in such a short time.

- She is being limited in scope as a means of diminishing her ability to contribute, which in turn will ultimately provide reason for discharge. Given this environment, I would begin to use stronger counter measures. I would now formally lodge a complaint with HR summarizing the above in a chronological fashion and perhaps solicit the EEOC or an outside lawyer to file a charge on her behalf-don't know if either will work but the end game here is no longer an extended stay at the company.

- This will get uncomfortable, but hopefully the duration is shorter verses longer. Once we have established our intent to push back and counter his approach, this sends the message that we are no longer a passive participant in the process, which in turn, begins to highlight his behavior and sheds some new light on it as well, since the potential to be accountable clearly has been defined-this will clearly signal the beginning of the end.

- From here, the question now becomes how should we proceed? Is this a feasible approach or better than the one we have been using? Is the trail convincing enough to show cause and effect (hero to zero)? Does he appear to be taking a retaliatory approach and can we make the case? What is it worth to the Company to make this go away, or will they use it as a "landmark" like case to show solidarity around their senior leadership team? At what point do they say just make this go away? All of these thoughts run through our mind as we contemplate next steps.

STRATEGY FINALIZATION

- Our friend, the lawyer, states he knows these are all questions I can't answer, but his biggest concern here is if we continue to passively rebut his comments, Judy continues to be drawn out as the person he is trying to characterize versus the person that received the top review score, gold award and inclusion in the mentor program. I think that positive base is the cornerstone of our case, and I see it slowly fading to black as time progresses.

- Our friend, the employment lawyer- I tend to agree with your suggestions here. You have it pegged right. There is not a good reason she is hero to zero overnight absent some insidious reason from Dick. My view is that Judy has to exit the organization one way or the other. That was my view from the beginning. I had hoped she could maintain her presence there while looking for another role somewhere else (easier to find a job when you have a job). It is apparent now that she may not have the choice to stay if the current situation takes it natural path. Lodging a formal complaint is a good idea but be prepared for the consequences (possible ostracization, possibly they send Judy home on suspension or to another job etc.). Or worse, they turn on her. Will they allow her to separate with a severance? Possibly, yes, but you need to lodge a complaint first and then possibly raise it with them. An attorney is a possibility.

- My Comment after the fact "Well they chose to turn on me. The worst case scenario occurred."

- Our friend further comments that, "I think if she is ready, she should escalate this thing asap". Whether HR is her friend here or not remains to be seen. But she has to have someone step in here. I would consider writing a letter to the president of the company as another option but that will piss off everyone else at a lower level. She would make it clear in her complaint to HR that this behavior is unwarranted and not professional, and she will escalate the matter if needed.

- The end strategy is she has to leave.

Our Friends response continues:

- I have thought about both steps. I think we need to see the next move from the Company before we chart the path for one or both of those options. An attorney might be too soon for them at this time. But if no good response comes, then I would consider it, yes.

- My husband states Judy is gone for vacation with her sister for a week. She has a meeting with the head of the mentor program when she gets back. His question to Judy was "what do you want out of this?" He shares my plan was to share that I wanted to stay there and return to doing quality work. It is still not clear to me who will eventually push this issue on her behalf inside HR, so we are in a wait and see mode, but with continued focus on now pushing the issue within the company in an attempt to follow protocol.

- Oddly though, in her last interrogation with her boss prior to her vacation, he began to ask questions of Judy regarding whether she had made some comments, and if so, who had she talked to in HR and what did she talk to them about. Very weird, since the line of questioning is out of line and secondly, I sense a level of uncomfortableness in his approach that leads me to believe that perhaps his hand is not as strong outside of his inner circle as we thought early on.

- On Friday, May 8 my boss calls in sick with fever over 100 degrees and aches and pains…yet comes in the next day. Interesting because he had asked me to come in for a meeting with him. He looked perfectly fine when he left. It looks like the 2-minute warning has begun. Judy is meeting with HR today.

- She plans to stick with the plan, she will not be going to any meetings with Dick, her boss, as they are intended to harass and intimidate her. The entire process has been run in a way to suggest he is trying to get rid of her and he is ruining her reputation within the company in the process. She will not tolerate that and wants fair treatment.

REACHING HIGHER – NOTIFYING THE CEO – MAY 12, 2009

As my lawyer friend had suggested earlier, we should consider writing a letter to the CEO/President to understand the values and culture of the company. I decided to write a letter to the CEO of the company, knowing there could be repercussions. Based on how aggressively my boss was documenting me, we felt that I didn't have much to lose. Plus, the plan was to address in person what occurred with Adam so this was not addressed in the letter to the CEO. It was addressed with HR numerous times. This was my letter:

To: Name and CEO, Company's Name
From: Judy Foley, "*Specific Organization* "Sourcing
Subject: Request for Meeting

My name is Judy Foley and I work at our corporate offices here in Chicago. It is with great personal disappointment that I am now compelled to reach out to your office and request a meeting to review ongoing unprofessional and retaliatory actions being taken against me by my direct manager. These aggressive tactics began in the January/February time frame and coincided with my questioning related to the integrity of a hiring process that was formally completed at that same time. Additionally, I have had commentary that I had included in our annual employee compliance and ethics "tone at the top" survey played back to me on more than one occasion indicating to me that I am also be subjected to punitive actions as a result of voicing my opinion within the survey itself. As a result of these actions I am systematically being set-up to fail despite my efforts to resolve this issue due to the positional power and control working against me.

As a backdrop to my request to meet and thoroughly review this situation, I think it is also fair to ask the question "who is this person" behind this letter. I am sourcing professional with 26 years of experience (4 at this company) that is highly regarded by my internal clients for the work I complete on their behalf. I work hard to make things happen, I hit my project dates on time, and at times, have pushed others to see that commitments are met. Prior to the events described above, I received a score of 1 on my 2008 performance review, I was the recipient of the Company's Gold Award prior to the onset of these issues, and I am a participant in the company's mentor program. I can assure you that my approach towards my work has not changed in less than three months. I remain a dedicated employee that only wants to continue contributing at a high level.

In closing, I've read multiple times the letter sent by you this past week highlighting the values that you working to build here at the company – understanding our customers, acting with integrity, communicating honestly, and working together to win. I believe in those values, and have tried to emulate them in my work here at the company. Writing this letter is by far the most difficult thing I have ever done in my professional career, but what is occurring is very wrong. No one deserves to be treated as I have, and my own personal integrity and sense of purpose tells me that allowing this to continue without escalating it is in effect a passive way of showing support for it. This issue needs to be addressed, and it is my belief that a review by your office represents the most likely solution to resolving this matter.

Respectfully Submitted,
Judy Foley

MEETING WITH COMPANY'S EMPLOYMENT LAWYER MAY 2009

The CEO's office referred me to meet with the company's employment lawyer. I discussed my concerns at the forefront as noted below. At the end of the meeting, I asked for a severance package. The lawyer asked, "Why would we give a #1 top employee a package?" Initially, her remarks in the meeting lead me to believe me there will be an investigation, and that we would work together.

CONCERNS AT THE FOREFRONT WITH COMPANY'S EMPLOYMENT LAWYER
AND HR REPRESENTATIVES

- Share my story of what occurred with Adam for celebration and establishing boundaries as documented

- I am an excellent employee that has been dedicated to the Company for the 4 years I have been here and my performance shows it.

  - Gold award

  - Received #1 in my performance review

  - Worked 70-80 hours to make the Supplier Management Organization happen for Company due to my dedication to the company

  - Nominated in the high-performance mentor program and assigned a senior vice president as my mentor for the year

- I have never been a poor performing employee for Dick to tell me how to do my job.

- This is not right and should not be allowed to continue! This is an intolerable situation.

- Dick is out to ruin my reputation and has begun the process to isolate me and eliminating my ability to complete the work I need to do.

  - Setting me up

  - He is harassing me because I am a woman and for some reason considers me a threat

  - He is there to intimidate and harass me

  - He is defaming me to my colleagues

  - He is creating an intolerable situation that is unacceptable.

- He has stated he will win at this game. I was not aware we were playing a game, but whatever game he thinks is being played must now stop and I expect this to be resolved.

- There is no reason to meet with Dick as he is up to no good and he is only out to hurt me, not help me. I do not plan to meet with him as there is no value if he continues to degrade me.

- I asked for another position where I could be successful and contribute to the organization. If this were impossible, I requested to receive a package while I looked for another job.

- I am looking for resolution to this overall issue.

The employment lawyer set up a meeting for me with Human Resources. HR interviewed me for four hours about my meeting with Adam. I heard the same questions and gave the same answers but it seemed to me that they expected my responses to change. I said" I felt like a rape victim. I kept telling the same story over and over but nothing had been done." I felt that they were not hearing me, but instead looking for inconsistencies.

I felt like I was facing a team of HR people who were not listening but just protecting the company – not me, their employee.

I had at least 8 meetings in May with HR where they questioned me. Some were one on one meetings and others were three people present. Same information shared with the Internal Employment Lawyer and any new issues that came up on harassment or other key points were addressed with HR.

I also meet with the HR contact who works in the division with Adam and was responsible for the mentor program. He did not provide any support or help me either. Consequently, I felt like I was facing a team of HR people who were not listening but just protecting the company – not the employee.

I asked a friend in HR in December 2008, if her responsibility would be to the company if there were a lawsuit, and she said yes. I basically gave them a heads up that something was coming. This was way before the EEOC suit was even filed. Big mistake from a strategy perspective. I always believed the right thing would be done and shared information that could have helped my case. The right thing being done was all I ever wanted. She did reach out to me a few times during this painful situation. We met at a restaurant when people were going after me strongly. When we sat down, she placed her satchel on the middle of the table, and it appeared to have a recording device in it. I lost respect for her over time as I thought she would do the right thing, yet she fully represented the company.

She was suggesting we connect on LinkedIn after I left. I told her if you had anything to do with what I went through at the company, do not connect with me on LinkedIn. She never connected.

NO SUPPORT FROM HR OR MANAGEMENT – MAY 2009-MARCH 2010

By the end of May, the internal employment lawyer asked my boss's boss, Executive VP and Chief Administrative Officer for HR to speak with the CEO. I told the internal employment lawyer that Dick's behavior was unacceptable in his emails and one-on-one meetings. In fact, the retaliation became even more elevated and harsh and continued even after I engaged HR to support me. I believed that those were not the actions of someone who is interested in keeping a number-one rated employee in this organization. I struggled to understand why HR continued to lightly dismiss the reality of my day-to-day work environment. I will never forget how this employment lawyer did everything she could to get me to fold over time, to agree with their statements about me, tried to get me to sign documents that were untrue and allow my boss and others to work to discredit me over time. What she did instead was to make me see that truth does not override evil, and she was going to work to win for the *company.*

GETTING A NEW EMPLOYMENT LAWYER INVOLVED — JUNE 2009

Once Legal action began, I noticed that if I was in a big department meeting for division, Adam saw I was there and he left immediately. I assumed legal had stated to him if she is in a meeting you must leave.

As discussed with our friend and lawyer, earlier, it was time for me to get our own legal counsel as this was taking up a lot of time for our friend who was in charge of legal counsel and responsible for the global needs of his company. My friend, the employment lawyer, connected me to a law firm that worked with employment issues. I was told to organize all the information I'd collected, starting with the big picture of who I was, my accomplishments, my work with Adam and what occurred with Adam. Then, I was to describe the jobs posted/filled late last year, how I questioned that, and Dick's reaction and actions taken after this. Also, I spent days going through emails to establish a chronological order for the meeting

We followed through on introductions. I met with two women lawyers and was a bit nervous about taking this step. I came with two large books of documentation completed and tabbed for the lawyers. They were surprised at the level of documentation and organization. They would review this later. They needed to hear what had occurred to determine if they would take my case.

They led the conversation and I answered what questions they asked of me. I was very honest sharing everything that had occurred with me at this company from the beginning when I started there to now. The experience with Adam was important. I found it interesting some of things that I said were important per a lawyer's perspective. Example that "*this area* was a man's world. "They said your boss said this to you. "Yes." I went on with my story. I answered the questions asked of me as one of them would ask me to explain this further or who said that. I broke down crying over some of the details. Did I ever expect that I would need to be going to a lawyer's office about my work? Never!

I was there for a couple of hours and answered their questions all throughout. I never documented what I stated but they certainly documented the whole time. I shared the good, the bad and the ugly but all of it was truthful.

COMPANY NOTIFIED OF LEGAL COUNSEL IN JUNE 2009

In early June, Dick began assigning my work to others and under-mining my plans for the supplier management project. My friend, the employment lawyer agreed that Dick was trying to force me out, and more than likely did not appreciate working with a woman that he perceived as a threat.

On June 8, I met with the head of employee relations. First, she told me there would be no package, but she'd watch for other jobs and would put me in touch with a recruiter. This never happened. All talk no action. She took Dick's side on everything. She told me she didn't think I was doing my part, and that if I didn't find a way to work with him, it would become an insubordination issue. She said she had seen Dick improve his communication – to me, it seemed as if she were insinuating that I hadn't done the same. When I described the harassing behaviors he was exhibiting, she basically disregarded me and went on stating her own case.

When we discussed the peculiarities of the job posting, she told me they had followed "normal procedures," and said I was welcome to apply for any job I wanted yet no one had even told me the job was posted. Her conclusion, after talking to Dick and HR, was that there were no integrity issues with the job posting.

On June 26, my employment lawyer contacted the company, saying they would be representing me and providing an overview of the case (the letter was more than 10 pages long). The employment lawyer shared Ms. Foley has provided me information regarding her employment with the company. I must be candid and state that I am deeply troubled by facts that Ms. Foley has been working in a discriminatory and retaliatory atmosphere and that company's intention is to make it so unbearable for her at the company that she will resign. While Ms. Foley enjoys her job with company (apart from her adverse treatment) and is clearly good at what she does, she recognizes that management at the Company no longer wants her to succeed or stay. Also, they addressed working together collaboratively and asked for copies of all my personnel files (hiring, promotions, assignment, evaluation, bonuses, stock options, and any other employment actions or decisions plus all of my complaints addressed with HR and Employee relations). The company was told to preserve any electronic messages regarding me. Despite counsel's involvement and my record of complaints, management was allowed to continue to campaign and denigrate my performance and reputation.

After my company received this letter, they hired an outside lawyer, a member of the National Labor and Employment Law Steering Committee and National Chairperson of its Complex Discrimination Litigation Practice Group. This woman lawyer had won favorable jury verdicts in the context of EEOC patterns, individual terminations, and harassment allegations. In other words, they were ready for a fight and the corporation had deep pockets to continue this fight.

EVALUATIONS – JULY/AUGUST 2009

On August 7, 2009, I submitted my self-evaluation as part of the mid-year checkpoint review process, highlighting my numerous contributions to that point in the year. I added this:

"Despite encountering efforts to undermine my reputation and isolate me from certain groups to which I previously contributed, my drive level and commitment to my teams and to the company has not diminished. I am proud of the work I have done and the way I professionally handled the challenges put before me. I remain hopeful that I will be given a fair opportunity to contribute my knowledge and skills, and a fair opportunity to succeed.

I am someone who constantly pushes to improve myself and reach new goals and experiences. For example, I recently took my first parachute jump. I realize I can do anything I set my mind to accomplish so long as I am given the same support and opportunities to succeed that others are given."

In the end my boss attempts to downgrade me in my review and does not consider any of the facts provided on what has been accomplished.

I was determined with the parachute jump to step out of my comfort zone and not allow fear to stop me from growing. Work was unpredictable and it was important to have the skills and confidence to face the issues head on. Knowing that I needed to be able to overcome insurmountable odds would build my confidence and reinforce my independence of who I was at the time.

On August 12, I responded to both attacks on my performance, detailing inaccuracies in management's assessment of my collaboration efforts. Recall in February, I am being recognized for my collaborative skills "Looking forward to continued collaboration in the future." Even though I had demonstrated that the management mid-year checkpoint review and my July performance document was not fair nor an accurate assessment of my contributions, the assessments did not change. I shared all of my accomplishments to date but this did not matter. Also, in August, the charge of sex discrimination and harassment were filed with the EEOC. At that point Dick took further steps to undermine my performance and career.

On October 13, 2009, I was placed on a 30-day Performance Improvement Plan (PIP). In that document, I was further critiqued for communication and teaming behaviors, which were false accusations, and I was criticized for delayed submission of my expenses and personal printing (as noted earlier that my mentor, senior vice president laughed about). Also, my boss needs to manage and give approval for all new projects which exceed 2 hours of work time.

On October 23, 2009, I provided a detailed response to the PIP documents, describing that I was being targeted for negative performance feedback as compared to my peers because I had raised concerns about discriminatory and retaliatory conduct by Adam and Dick. Despite my disagreement with the criticisms in the PIP document, as a professional, I continued to demonstrate an unwavering commitment to my clients, peers, and superiors and to the objectives they were trying to attain as stated in my August 7th self-evaluation.

On November 17, 2009, I was notified that I had met the terms of the PIP and that my performance rating would be changed. Lawyers addressed the 2 rating (meets all requirements) versus the company's position of placing me at a rating level of 3 (meets most requirements). From February 2009 through April 2009, I was at a 1 (exceeding all requirements). I was requested to sign this PIP update document but **never did**, as the information was not accurate and was established by my boss. I told him where the inaccuracies existed but the document was never updated. Basically, the document said there were no further issues, and I had met the requirements.

My lawyers told me *not* to sign anything, and I did not sign anything. The lawyers said, "You have to be perfect, or they will find a reason to let you go." My success would depend on documenting meetings, actions, and results by dates and people assigned to complete them. This was something I had always done based on my project management experience. I needed to be very thorough in my documentation.

Since the end of December, I was required to train individuals on what I had been doing and teaching them my process. I weathered the unfounded attacks on my performance, ending in 2009 with a favorable PIP, the damage to my reputation at the company which was palpable and unacceptable.

Around February 11, 2010, I complained in writing to my boss, Dick, about the disparately negative treatment I was receiving from management on the basis of my sex. The next day, I was requested to send Dick a summary of my projects and goals and shared concerns about the number of assignments going to my peer. Now my peer, appears to be accepted as a part of the good ol' boys club and appears he was doing what was requested of him. The same guy that Adam would not work with due to his lack of strategy capabilities. He is targeting me by his actions and feeling quite comfortable in doing so as a member of the ol' boys club. I shared Dick had become hostile in meetings as well, and HR continued to do nothing about either situation. By doing nothing HR was condoning it.

TERMINATION – MARCH 2010

While I weathered the barrage of unfounded attacks on my performance, the damage to my status and reputation was palpable. As I began establishing my goals and objectives for 2010, it became clear that a number of the key initiatives – for which I was well qualified – were being assigned to the man who was once unable to create the strategy or meet Adam's requirements.

Less than three weeks after I wrote that summary, on March 1, 2010, I was fired. I specifically stated to Dick and the new HR representative, "that she should be looking at Dick more closely as he lacked a level of integrity commensurate with his position." Dick had not given me any written performance feedback since notifying me of the successful completion of the November 2009 PIP issues. The HR representative stated that I was fired because of the October 2009 PIP. The lack of any performance documentation demonstrating that I had failed to sustain a satisfactory performance in the months between the end of PIP and my termination was extremely telling.

After telling me that I was fired, I was told I was not allowed to go back to my desk. I was notified that the company would send my belongings from my desk to my home. To humiliate me even further, they wanted to retrieve my coat for me from my office! I refused and was allowed to get my own coat, but they warned me not to say anything to anyone along the way. They tried to make feel like a criminal when, in fact, my boss was the one lacking in character and integrity.

EEOC FILING

When my lawyers filed my case with the Equal Employment Opportunity Commission, they highlighted how I had been subjected to unlawful sex discrimination, harassment and retaliation in violation of Title VII of the Civil Rights Act of 1964. They further summarized all of the key points I had also made to the HR staff regarding my work performance, the hostile work environment, and the implied quid pro quo sexual advances of the person who ultimately began the informal campaign of denigrating my performance and value to the organization. While the case was eventually was retired without a formal admission of guilt by the organization, it served only to reinforce the efforts and structure in place to support this behavior by those with larger titles and power. The system served to shield the behaviors of practices of those in authority rather than help those most in need. Perhaps my largest mistake was not to notify HR when this first issue occurred, but in retrospect, the HR team and the system they represented would more than likely have accelerated my departure rather than supported it. It is the infrastructure built upon these biases that works against us, and the system must change in order to secure a more diverse workforce and a higher level of integrity.

AFTERMATH AND HEALING

When this was over, every piece of me knew that I needed to heal, and telling my story was part of the process. If I was unable to do that, I just couldn't go on any further. They say that you change when your back is against the wall – that was true in this case. The toughest decision we face is not about success or failure but to simply try again.

In every other part my life, change had been easy. I am usually a change agent, and I have made change happen in my career and family, yet I felt I had now become a financial burden to my husband and family who love me so much. They recalled how happy I was about life, how I loved my job, and how I loved my husband and children.

In late 2017, my oldest son said, "Mom, before what happened to you at the company you were so dedicated to the company, you were the happiest person I knew. You loved your job and had such passion around your career and life. I've never met anyone who was as happy as you were."

You see, I have been suffering for 10 years – about eighteen months going through this ordeal and more than eight years trying to recover from retaliation for speaking my truth about sexual discrimination, harassment and retaliation. There was a time when I wondered whether I should take my life so the pain would stop. This is not like me, but it had come to this.

I turned to every type of help you can imagine, which has cost my family and husband a lot financially and personally. To help me get unstuck, I have seen counselors and pastors gone on a 10-day retreat of silence, looked to executive coaches, sought the help of healers, energy experts, and a spiritual advisor at a monastery who is an expert in trauma. I have taken many courses and seminars to make me top-of-my-game again and get that "right" company to offer me a job.

From this experience, I began to believe that there is an undercurrent that limits you in your job search, and you have a big red checkmark against you when you speak the truth and address it with everything you have. Would people say, "Oh yes, she accomplished a lot in every company she worked at, but let's not hire her because she spoke up on a major issue. What will she speak out on in *our* corporation?"

I have interviewed and been so close to so many opportunities. In the beginning, I was offered a chief of staff position with a large company, yet I wondered if I was being set up to fail as it was in the same industry. My trust was impacted at the company that fired me, and I wasn't sure if good ol' boys everywhere would continue to go after me.

Also, to add to the emotional issues, since this happened, I've been affected physically. I've had more surgeries and health issues than ever before. I have had the meniscus rip in both knees, my calf muscle ripped, hysterectomy, and knee replacement in both knees. I gained about 30 pounds and had no will power to lose it or achieve other goals that had been easy for me to do in the past. Medical experts suggest that chronic stress *can* directly impact the brain, leading to a chain of physiological responses – including chronic inflammation and cellular activity. It is amazing to me releasing this experience has allowed me to lose 15 lbs. and allow me to not carry the burden of this experience.

In reviewing my journals now, the same theme kept occurring. I was desperate to put this pain behind me, yet I could not. Initially, I relived it for 3 years, every day and had a pain in my heart that would not go away. I worked with a family counselor during the experience and after for a period of time. An expert at that 10-day retreat taught me this: "It is what it is." In other words, you can't change what happened, and you must accept it – one more step toward healing.

I am (and was) such a strong, confident person, and in my heart, I don't understand why I haven't been able to let this go. Yet, there are basics in how I viewed life that have been turned upside down – that good will win over evil, and that a respected corporation would do the right thing. My trust in the world changed, and I wondered at that time how much the good ol' boys impacted me or would continue to.

My eyes have been opened to a world I'd never seen. I had trusted so much that I had never known the impact of *not* trusting until this happened. To not trust takes away such freedoms in life. I try to move on and move forward. But when I review just a portion of my notes from that time, it all comes flooding back. However, you must move forward until you can release the pain and make the experience a part of you and your life. I know I will use it to make a difference for others.

On my journey of healing, I have been exposed to very powerful leaders and professionals who share personal stories of their trials in their career or personal life. These people showed me other expertise or skills that I did not see in myself. It was a gift to me to meet these people, hear their stories, and see my skill sets from others' views and expertise. I appreciated their stories, as they made me realize that they too had had experiences that were not what they expected – and learned from them.

I also met other individuals with different outlooks. Some were all about themselves, their accomplishments, and doing whatever it took to get ahead. Some were men and women who cheated on their spouses and chased temporary happiness. But I've also met very accomplished people who are making a difference in the world, not just for themselves but for others. I have seen those who need to find their way on their own path. Others have given up on their dreams. Yet I believe we all make a difference in the world through our experiences.

What I know from all of this is that no one's life is perfect, and when someone makes it appear so, know there have been obstacles along the way that got them to where they are. The key is to establish our priorities annually and never lose focus, even when those obstacles appear. We must take accountability for our lives, achieve happiness, follow through on daily appreciation, and never give up on ourselves or the people we love. For me, believing in a higher power was key. I could not have made it without my faith in God and the support of my family!

I have been truly blessed over my lifetime, and I can say there were bumps along the way. My biggest bumps were my death of my father and the experience I describe in this book. My mother helped us through the death of my father. I always believed that the death of a loved one usually listed #1 as the highest stressful life event, that I had come through this well and I could handle anything. Yet dealing with this experience at the company far outweighs it. My husband, family, and friends have helped me through this tough time. Most of my friends did not know the exact issue of dealing with sexual discrimination, harassment, and retaliation because I was told by a HR Coach that I should not share it as it would hurt me in finding jobs. I now know it prolonged my healing process.

I have led an amazing life. My husband for 35 years and now ex-husband, is my best friend and a wonderful father to our children.

He has always had high integrity and I share a trust with him that most people never experience, a love that was special, and a friendship that means the world to me. I will never forget his support during the worst of times. We brought different strengths to the marriage that I believe helped balance the life that our children were exposed to in the influencing years and even today. This experience changed me forever and the person I was, would never be again. I am sure the same occurred for my husband and children. Yet growth for me and my family will occur as we move forward.

I have learned that everyone is on their own journey. I have been judgmental about what is right and wrong, but I now know that I can determine what is right for me. I will probably always struggle with right and wrong for my family. Others must decide what is right for them and learn along the way, just as I have learned. There are nuggets of gold in learnings from others and our experiences. I urge you to take the risk to share your stories with others. Your experiences may help others overcome the same difficulties.

CHAPTER 3

WHAT WAS THE PERSONAL EXPERIENCE LIKE FOR ME?

"Workplace sexual harassment thrives in a culture of silence,
but companies should understand the risks of fostering
this type of environment."

—Unknown

COMPANY EXPERIENCE

First of all, it destroyed trust in this company. The values the company said were theirs were not followed through on in their actions. I admired my boss and quickly learned he was not the person I respected and he did not have integrity. He did whatever was necessary to protect this executive rather than standing for what the company said they stood for.

The CEO to whom I addressed a letter explaining who I was; noting my accomplishments achieved; wanting to meet with him based on his open-door policy and the fact that politics were working against me. Instead he closed that door. He did the direct opposite of what he had said a week before in a quarterly meeting with the company about his open-door policy. My friend who was the head of employment law for a large global company said this letter will tell us what the culture of this company is. Boy did it ever! Instead I was sent to the employment lawyer who was a woman. My friend and lawyer had prepared me to ask for a package, her response was why would we give a #1 employee a package?

The lack of professionalism that occurred within the company was horrific. I was questioned by an HR representative for about 4 hours about the celebration of achievements with Adam. I remember saying to the individual, "You keep asking me the same questions my responses will not change. I feel like a rape victim, I keep telling my story to different people and no one seems to hear it." I felt like a victim that was not being heard and they were trying to twist everything. The ongoing approach by HR was unacceptable.

ISSUES CREATED FROM THIS COMPANY EXPERIENCE

1 Trust loss in a company

2 Trust loss in management

3 Values of the company were not upheld

4 Impact to others as people did see things were not right and I was being taken down.

   a One woman told me in my department do not work with this area.

   b Questions came up all of the time?

      i You are a star. You will go no where but up from here. What's going on?

   ii   People taking responsibility for what I had done or what I had done with a team of people.

       1   Woman director that did not have the skills, stood in front of organization and took the accomplishment and made it her own.

       2   She presented details that were not correct and I shared in that meeting what the team had actually done.

       3   My boss was not happy that I corrected the facts and results.

  iii Eliminating me from meetings. Others asking, how come you were not in this meeting?

  iv The woman, Claudia who was now in the role calling people and wanting issues reported to my boss about me.

       1   The people who were my friends tried to not address them as they did not feel they were issues. Until the woman would say, "did this get reported to her boss?"

       2   My boss was the mentor to this woman. I found this to be an interesting fact that she shared this with me.

   v Negative things being said to impact my reputation in larger staff meetings within the division that Adam worked and my boss placing a representative from Procurement in the meeting (a person getting her law degree).

  vi Communicating to staff questionable statements as they brought them back to me and did not understand what was occurring.

1   One of executive's direct staff came to me and said you are on probation. When I asked further questions, he clammed up. He said he had opened his mouth and should not say stupid things.

vii Needing to summarize everything I was working on and training people to take on my responsibilities.

viii Training people on processes and procedures I established for my RFP's and helping them understand how to get results like I had.

5   I did not know if the good ol' boys would stop even after I left the company.

   a   I went to an executive that I knew from another company I had worked at and shared a 5-minute synopsis of what happened. I asked would they stop, he said he hoped so. He was not sure.

   b   He also shared that any company would protect an executive just like this company had done. This scared me as I thought what company can you trust. I did not believe this could happen not in my experience of good overriding evil.

6   Spiritually I believed in God. This was critical to me being able to stay strong. I went over every day across the street to a catholic church when I was Lutheran to pray and ask for guidance.

   a   I believe this company had been doing this to women for many years. The feedback shared within my own organization was the following:

      i   In meetings I was involved in with the division there were comments stated or snickering amongst the guys on what some of the women stated on the teleconference calls. They sometimes placed the phone on hold and would state a comment about the woman and move on. Never ever saw them do this to men.

ii   In my case, I had a woman share she had an issue that went to HR years ago and was told we will hold your complaint overnight and if you do not return tomorrow morning, we will assume you have dropped your issue. She felt if she returned her job was at stake so she did not return the next morning.

iii   Another situation I was made aware of was a gay person was addressed by the Management as "all of the girls are here" when he came in with other women.

iv   An older woman in my department warned me to not work in this area, but she didn't say much more. I shared that I have enjoyed my work and am excited about taking on new responsibilities. Later, when she became aware of a problem, she says, "I told you not to take a job in this area." From her comment, I got the impression I was not the only one who has had this issue...possibly many over the years.

v   When I left the company, a retired HR executive told me that this company has had this reputation for years. I responded that I wished I had known, as I would have made a different decision about working for this company. I also said that I had enjoyed about three years there and had never known this type of action occurred in businesses. It was so disappointing as I had accomplished so much at this company and loved working with the people.

b   I also knew God gave me strength to speak the truth throughout my life and this was my calling.

c I remember praying to God in the church out loud as I was the only one there this day: If I sign a Nondisclosure agreement no one will hear this story and if you want me to write this story then I am not to sign. I leave it in your hands.

    i God requested that I write the book a year before the "Me Too "and "Times Up" movement began. I was not ready and it took one more year before I was willing to start writing the book.

d At the end of this experience at the company, I was exhausted emotionally. Yet I held my head high as I had kept my integrity.

e Writing this story in 2019 has helped to heal the scars produced from the experience.

f Unacceptable that a company would do this to an individual, women or any other group.

    i Recovery was difficult. It took me three years to go back to work and relived experience for 3 years.

    ii Initially when going back to work I had no passion for the work I once loved and had post-traumatic stress disorder (PTSD) that I needed to overcome. I needed to focus on my past reaction to verbal attacks and abusive behavior that occurred and establish post traumatic growth from the experience.

    iii Consulting allowed me to be in control and manage work conditions.

PERSONAL EXPERIENCE

I was a very positive, happy person. I had always seen the positive side of the world. My family was directly impacted by this experience. Every night my husband and I discussed what had occurred during the day and discussed the plan for the next day until one night my youngest child, 15 years old, stood up to say he was going to destroy my boss's computer for what he was doing. We shared that he could not do this and explained why. Both him and my husband were my nights in shining armor. The whole family (daughter, my other son, sister, brothers, mom) wanted to protect me and was seeing what it was doing to me.

Also, during this time my husband sent me on multiple trips at the end to be able to handle all of the retaliation and be prepared for the next retaliation. My husband worked non-stop due to the fact we knew my job would be going away. This started after Labor Day 2008 and continued until March 2010. I tried to resolve this myself until December 2008. I was naïve to think I could resolve but I believed the truth and facts would override what was occurring. The company's harassment and retaliation were getting more harried in their approach with me.

Also, they needed me for the Supplier Management Organization initiative so they used me during this time as I understood the whole project and oversaw so many aspects of what was occurring. In December, my husband suggested I address everything that was occurring with our friend who was a top employment lawyer. Being our friend had such global responsibilities we had gone from daily meetings to weekly Sunday meeting and if issues came up, he made himself available.

Around end of May we started working with another lawyer our friend recommended. During this time, they attempted to take me from a #1 employee to a #3 employee. The lawyers had fought this with #2 meets requirements. My lawyers said any mistakes will mean they will find a way to use this to get rid of you. I realized at this point anything can be done in a company and it does not need to be factual. My boss brought up issues and said people were complaining. I started checking on these issues and being able to address the true story in the multiple meetings they had for me daily. My boss would shrink and say we will discuss this later as now I was showing his facts to not be true. Then the company's employment lawyer stated I could not go to these people to ask questions that I needed to let my boss understand the facts. This was truly death but they barred me from doing this anymore.

ISSUES CREATED FOR ME AND MY FAMILY PERSONALLY

1 Every night we had to strategize for the next day. It took time away from the family.

2 Also, I needed to document for the lawyers what was occurring each night.

3 My husband and I had always been involved in our children's lives. I was very involved before all of this happened yet my husband had to step up even more to take on more responsibility with the kids.

4 This was not a good experience and it took everything to stay positive.

5 We did less with friends as I was not myself. I am generally a person that does a lot of entertaining and I reduced this significantly. We generally did this every Saturday night and sometimes on Sunday based on the children's activities. We reduced who we saw during this time and after this occurred primarily because of how I felt.

6   My husband and I had always gone out on Friday nights as date night. We eliminated this as we could see my job would be going away from a fund's perspective.

7   My children saw me originally as the happiest person they ever knew and this rolled into all of our lives. I worked to stay as positive as I could.

8   My husband received a call from me every day and he could not even believe what was occurring. He would discuss strategy with me and somehow made time for me when he had big responsibilities himself. I can never say how much, I appreciate he was there for me every step of the way.

9   Also, originally at night we would strategize over dinner. Our younger son was 15 years old. One day he pushed his chair back, rose up and said I have had it, I am going to break your boss's computer.

    a   My husband and I then realized; we could not talk about this further over dinner. We discussed every night but not where the kids would hear the strategy. One child was in college and the two were in high school when this was occurring. Towards the end we had two children in college and one in high school.

10   After I lost my job, I did not know who to trust. I interviewed and would get to the end like I was going to get the job and some weird questions would come up. Example interviewed with California Company, same industry. The woman head of the department let me know all was going well and she was talking like I was joining them. Started sharing my responsibilities and some inside information about organization. I meet with the CFO and he does not understand why someone so

good would be let go with an organizational change based on how I was told to address. He kept digging in and I felt he had connected to the good old boy network at the company.

11 Also offered a Chief of Staff Job with another major Company, same industry. I would need to go out to east coast in one of two locations, where cost of living was higher at my current pay, live there for the week and then come home to my family on the weekends. I could not do it without my family and miss out on their lives. Also, I did not know if I was being set up by the good old boys again.

   a   Being able to trust was impacted and I had to work to override my experience.

12 Something that I thought was weird I would not let go of the documentation from this experience. I mean boxes of detail. It took me years to release some of this and yet I kept documentation to substantiate everything I had done over my professional life. I felt if I needed to prove what I had done that I had the detail based on the lies produced by management at this company.

13 Everyone would say to me how I was so talented yet I could not get a job. I felt like a scarlet letter had been placed on me. Not sure how companies do this but they have some way to communicate amongst themselves.

14 I now see, I never recovered from this experience. I liked consulting because it allowed me more control on who I worked with and to manage circumstances if I ever had to address them again.

15 Also, this experience impacted my physical and mental health.

   a   I had to fight to stay positive and keep looking for the right career opportunity.

b Physically I had to deal with a lot of surgeries at the time and I believe it was related to the stress I was under from this experience

    i I had the meniscus rip in both knees, my calf muscle rip, hysterectomy and knee replacement in both knees.

16 My experience impacted my marriage and family as I was working to recover and it took me ten years to do that.

a I had 18 months of going through the experience at the company and over 8 years to recover.

17 My husband stood by my side, yet financially this impacted us in every way. He is now my ex-husband that I am best of friends with.

a I now know I needed to survive and put all of my effort into coming out whole.

b My ex-husband is an amazing man that I will love forever. His integrity, support and friendship have been a gift to me. I wish I could see all of this with everything I was going through. I could never understand when I knew this, why I could not be there for him and needed to work on my recovery. I needed to work on being whole again. Is this related to trauma?

Trauma Expert: In terms of your above paragraph, I think is related to being a woman in the culture that as Estes (Women who Run with the Wolves) notes, when a woman is called home she must go. And she must stay as long as she needs to. In the culture women are always taking others into account until something calls them home. This is different for men. They do not do quite the same thing nor are they socialized to include others in the same way. They are socialized to be for themselves. This is why he could potentially be there for you which is good but you needed to focus on you and all that was. Men also do not usually have these experiences and if they are in a similar situation it is somewhat different. I also think this was/is a spiritual call for you. And you needed to do it as you did. Your question is interesting in that it refers to 'not doing it right' which could be related to a trauma learning.

    i   Example: On the plane you put oxygen on you first before you worry about another loved one next to you. I needed my oxygen to survive.

18 I had a choice to pursue suing the company yet we would need to take money from our savings. Did I chance our nest egg and our children's college or was its time to let it go? I chose to let it go as I could not make our family pay any more than what we had been through already. Plus, the company was ready to fight and they had deep pockets.

    a   I cried when my lawyer shared that I could sue yet this could be high in cost as company had deep pockets and plans to fight you.

CHAPTER 4

HOW DOES SEXUAL HARASSMENT PLAY OUT IN TODAY'S WORLD

"The high road for a woman for centuries was silence.
The new high road is speaking up."

—Zoe Saldana told Cosmopolitan rules have changed
in the Film Industry and #MeToo (Sexual Harassment)

The "Times Up" Movement began and initially started with Harvey Weinstein in the movie industry. On the Time's Up movement website is a statement that reads, "The clock has run out on sexual assault, harassment, and inequality in the workplace. It's time to do something about it." Times Up legal defense was initiated to defray legal and public relations costs for select cases of harassment and retaliation in the work place. "According to the National Women's Law Center (NWLC) which administers the fund, about 40% of those requesting help are women of color and 65% of them are low-income, from industries like construction, food services, and the military." [1]

Per website, since launching…

- More than 3400 women and men have been connected to legal resources through the TIME'S UP Legal Defense Fund.

- Two-thirds of those who contact the fund identify as low-wage workers.

- There are more than 800 attorneys in the network and top attorneys across the country are taking on the cases.

The "Me Too" campaign occurred in 2006 to help survivors of sexual violence. Tarana Burke, the founder of the "Me Too" movement has propelled the conversation on sexual violence and harassment into national and international dialogue. The #Me Too phrase was reignited because of the viral hashtag #metoo in October 2017, when allegations against Harvey Weinstein began to emerge. Actress Alyssa Milano tweeted: "If all the women who have been sexually harassed or assaulted wrote 'me too' as a status, we might give people a sense of the magnitude of the problem."

Since then, #MeToo has either been used as a statement of solidarity on social media, or attached to horrific accounts of harassment and abuse recorded by men and women. The volume of allegations of sexual harassment and sexual assault has begun to emerge, and were amplified and highlighted by a number of high profile women honored as Time's magazine 2017 Person of the Year as Silence Breakers. Also, the #MeToo movement has continued to vocalize that sexual harassment stands as an obstacle to the efficient allocation of human and financial capital. #MeToo continues to ripples through businesses, churches, government, schools and our society. A number of resignations, public firings, legal actions and other disciplinary measures have impacted the movie industry, business executives, politicians, churches and others. While it is often said that it takes three generations to change a culture, the focus of these programs has successfully created the momentum to accelerate this change in our society and workplace.

"Since 2017, a number of high-profile chief executives officers have resigned amid allegations of sexual harassment, including Mike Hurd of Hewlett Packard, Dove Charney of American Apparel, Roger Ailes of Fox News, Mark Light of Signet Jewelers, Kris Duggan of the enterprise software company betterworks, and Mike Cagney of the online lender Sofi, In addition, Uber founder Travis Kalanick resigned as CEO amid allegations that he tolerated a toxic work environment creating widespread sexual harassment that continued to perpetuate with his knowledge. These are just a few of the ones that have made headlines due to their high profile nature, however it is likely that we are seeing just the tip of the iceberg.

Corporate America has taken notice in recent months, leading to the departures of high-profile executives resulting in sharp stock price declines at a number of firms. Additionally, investors have also taken notice and exercised their legal rights as well. Shareholders at more than a half dozen publicly traded companies filed lawsuits since the start of 2017 alleging that corporate fiduciaries breeched state law duties or violated federal securities laws in connection with sexual harassment scandals. Additional suites are likely."[2]

The year 2017 marked a turning point in the evolution of sexual misconduct. Based upon the combined efforts of these two movements, the issues of sexual assault, sexual harassment and inequality in the workplace are beginning to be addressed. These issues needed to be brought to the forefront. Both women and men need to address these concerns and not continue to suffer in silence. The culture of companies and human resource staff focused on company support versus employee advocacy has allowed this silence to permeate and now needs to be resolved for companies to truly become world class. One incident of misconduct does not render a company's code of ethics misleading, yet a company that states ethical leadership despite knowledge of numerous wrong doing can subject itself to liability under the law.

WHAT CONSTITUTES SEXUAL HARASSMENT?

Sexual harassment is a form of *Sex Discrimination* that occurs in the workplace. Persons who are the victims of sexual harassment may sue under Title VII of the *Civil Rights Act of 1964* (42 U.S.C.A. § 2000e et seq.), which prohibits sex discrimination in the workplace.

Sexual harassment is generally divided into two categories. The first is unwelcomed sexual conduct that is either an explicit or implicit term or condition of employment, such as offering an employee a promotion or pay increase for agreeing to sexual demands or terminating an employee who refuses a sexual advance. This is known as quid pro quo (this for that) sexual harassment. For example, in the high-profile case involving Harvey Weinstein, Weinstein was accused of textbook quid pro quo sexual harassment by requesting sexual acts or favors from actresses and others in the entertainment industry in exchange for favorable treatment or roles.

The second form of sexual harassment is unwelcomed sexual conduct that unreasonably interferes (on purpose or in effect) with an individual's work performance or creates an intimidating, hostile, or offensive working environment. This is known as hostile or offensive work environment sexual harassment.

Harassing behavior can include sexual advances, requests for sexual favors, other verbal or physical conduct of a sexual nature, or offensive remarks about a person's appearance. While the recent accusations appear to primarily focus on sexual harassment directed at women, both men and women may be sexually harassed including sexual preference, and harassment can occur between members of the same sex.

WHY DO PEOPLE NOT REPORT SEXUAL HARASSMENT?

HARASSMENT IN THE WORKPLACE IS OFTEN UNREPORTED THAT ARE OFTEN DRIVEN BY FINANCIAL OR SOCIAL CONCERNS. HARASSED EMPLOYEES:

- Fear that their claim will not be believed or taken seriously. Worry about losing their job and the economic impact it can have on their family or those that rely on them.

- Worry about social and professional retaliation and the perception of others that can result in being ostracized and tagged as a trouble maker

- Harbor doubts about the confidentiality of internal grievances, and whether concerns voiced with be considered confidential and not later leaked or released.

- Are concerned that consequences of an investigation will be unsatisfactory to the employee, further discouraging reporting.

- Are uncertain of the sincerity of the company and whose best interest will they really represent and support.

- Will the organization blacklist you?

- Regardless of the reason, the fact remains that victims of harassment, rarely report the situation.

  - Per EEOC statistics, about 6% to 13% who experience harassment file a formal complaint

  - That means, on average, anywhere from 87% to 94% of individuals impacted by sexual harassment did not file a formal complaint.

WHAT IS THE IMPACT ON YOUR COMPANY?

Beyond the emotional impact inflicted upon employees attempting to work in a problematic environment, if your company becomes party to a lawsuit involving any type of workplace harassment, your costs could be enormous for litigation and liability. Litigation and the potential for a settlement against a firm can have an impact in many areas. Employees begin to question the ethics and integrity of the organization they are a part of, and external perceptions of actions taken can also create undue pressure on an organization. Stock price impacts, overall reputation of the firm and customer's separating to avoid guilt by association are all lasting results of a pubic settlement against a firm that doesn't maintain a fiduciary position in support of their employees.

Historically, some companies have believed that confidentiality agreements, non-disparagement clauses in settlements and now forced arbitration agreements - may save them from the actions of their employees and allow them to sweep sexual harassment under the rug without public dissemination. However, while these agreements have helped to protect a company's reputation and settle claims without going to trial, the environment is changing with transparency becoming the norm and the requirements of those with responsibility to manage and oversee corporate governance being held accountable for the culture and environment they oversee. The days of hiding behind agreements to avoid public oversight continue to decline as both employees and investors look for clarity and purpose in what they do or where they invest."[1]

WHAT IS THE IMPACT OF HARASSMENT ON YOUR EMPLOYEES?

- The ultimate impact of harassment for employee's in an organization that perpetuates this environment are personal discomfort as reviewed earlier, but reduced morale and productivity within the organization

- Organizations with the reputation of allowing sexual harassment to exist may have difficulty hiring new employees, incur high turnover rates, and establish a reputation that precedes them in what has become a competitive marketplace where potential employees have a great say in where and who they work for.

- It is imperative that a company take the necessary steps to prevent sexual harassment from occurring in the workplace and creating that safe haven for all employees.

- Policies and employee training are critical needs, but enforcement is the ultimate bellwether when issues occur.

- When harassment happens, it is up to the organization to respond courageously instead of scapegoating, wrongfully placing blame, or taking steps to wither and coverup the incident or retaliate against the victim.

- Companies need to respond properly as they risk watching years of good work impacted based on one employee's bad actions.

EXAMPLE: ROGER AILES, CEO FOR FOX NEWS

"The recent *ouster of Roger Ailes as the CEO of Fox News* speaks volumes about our partial progress on issues of sexual harassment in the workplace. For centuries, women were harassed without a name or a remedy for the problem. And when they experienced a "problem" with their supervisor, the problem was always theirs, not his. All that has changed, as Ailes's resignation reflects. But the fact that his behavior persisted over a quarter century, and involved, at least *25 women*, shows the progress yet to be made. For Ailes, like other abusers, his sexual harassment was only partly about sex; it was also about power.

Fox initially responded in a way *all too typical of employers in sex harassment cases*: shoot the messenger. Its public relations department went into high gear and strenuously denied the allegations, portrayed Carlson as a disgruntled employee with an ax to grind, released affectionate emails from Carlson to Ailes, and recruited other women at Fox News - came to his defense.

At the same time, the company's legal team sought to move Carlson's suit to arbitration, which would prevent other victims from publicly testifying on her behalf. Arbitration would also trigger the clause in Carlson's contract that puts a gag order on all facts related to the allegations, a clause heavily detailed and unusual in its level of protectiveness.

However, as the outcome in the Ailes case makes clear, when companies respond to sexual harassment the way Fox initially did, they ultimately pay the price in higher turnover, lower morale, legal fees, and reputational damage. Fewer and fewer women are willing to put up with anything like the abuses that Fox tolerated. Retaliation claims connected with allegations of discrimination *doubled between 1997 and 2015*, and now constitute the most common complaints made to the Equal Employment Opportunity Commission.

To some observers, cases like Ailes prompt an obvious question: What was he thinking? To experts on sex harassment, the answer seems equally obvious. He wasn't thinking. He didn't realize that he needed to. As Berkeley psychologist Dacher Keltner has shown, power can create a sense of entitlement and moral myopia that desensitizes people to how their actions injure others. The only way to check such tendencies is to create cultures of accountability in handling workplace complaints, and to protect victims against retaliation. As is typical in cases of workplace harassment, the tone set at the top often percolates throughout the organization.

To protect themselves, companies must rein in abusive behavior before it becomes corrosive. Arbitration and secrecy clauses won't do that."[3]

(Also, Refer to Chapter 8:" SuperStar" Harasser document by EEOC for additional information on this subject)

"Twenty-First Century Fox Inc reached a $90 million settlement of shareholder claims arising from the sexual harassment scandal at its Fox News Channel, which cost the jobs of longtime news chief Roger Ailes and anchor Bill O'Reilly. The settlement calls for insurers of Fox officers, Fox directors and Ailes' estate to pay the $90 million to the New York-based company for the benefit of shareholders."[4]

WE MUST STAND FOR TRUTH AND NOT ALLOW THIS TO CONTINUE. The cultures of organizations need to change to meet the needs of the total organization and diversified workforce that exists today.

COMPANY CULTURE IS CRITICAL

Does your company culture from the CEO and Board of Directors eliminate harassment or support it in their underlying culture? Over and over again, workplace culture has the greatest impact on allowing harassment to flourish or prevent harassment. Critical to the culture of the organization is leadership, accountability, and following through on values of the company.

1   Does the company's Board of Directors and CEO to have a commitment to a diverse, inclusive, and respectful workplace where harassment is not accepted nor tolerated?

2   Do all levels of management have systems in place that hold all employees accountable to the expectation that harassment in the work place is unacceptable?

3   Does your organization have a commitment to place a premium on diversity and inclusion strategy? This is key to a harassment free workplace.

4   All employees regardless of their race, religion, national origin, sex (including pregnancy, sexual orientation, or gender identity), age, disability or genetic information cannot be harassed on any of this basis.

You will *not* find out until you are attempting to address a concern, what your company's actions will be and whether they will be in line with their written values. The company will say harassment is not acceptable, yet when *you need* to address harassment, you will understand whether leadership, human resources and employment lawyers will follow through on an investigation to understand the facts, be objective and determine resolution that is appropriate. Retaliation is never acceptable by a company or representatives from a company.

CORPORATE CULTURE: IT STARTS AT THE TOP LEADERSHIP AND ACCOUNTABILITY ARE CRITICAL

The best way for companies to protect themselves and their workers is by changing the culture. Companies need to be proactive and intentional in creating the culture that treats employees with respect and dignity. Harassment must be forbidden and resolution must come from the top of the organization. Individuals who covet power and control will wield influence and a culture of silence can take hold as was evident in the Fox news case.

ESTABLISH ANTI-HARASSMENT POLICY

When establishing an Anti-Harassment Policy, consider for resources from the EEOC. Checklists from the Select Task Force on the Study of Harassment in the Workplace and Society for Human Resource Management provide guidance on creating policies and procedures. Additionally, review your state laws as specific requirements for these policies may be defined. A comprehensive program is essential for ensuring due diligence as an employer and addressing the employee's safety and well-being. It is the basis for employee communication and training, and should include your protocol for managing incidents reported. Management at all levels need to enforce the policies and ensure there is compliance and the plan is applied consistently. The EEOC has identified risk factors in harassment so your company can be proactive and consider these when designing or updating policies. (please see summary per checklist in Chapter 9)

TRAINING

It's important to get your workforce engaged in the process of learning and understanding harassment issues. Employees need to know that it's more than just getting sensitivity to the issues: it's about adhering to ethical standards, treating people with respect, and upholding the standards of your organization. Periodic training on harassment may be required for employers in some jurisdictions, but whether required or not, training and retraining helps reinforce your commitment to your employees' safety and well-being. Continuing education that's delivered over time and on an ongoing and recurring basis should include explaining responsibilities and expectations of all employees, training on situational awareness case studies to highlight both positive and negative behaviors, and creating an understanding of the different types of harassment.

SOURCES

1. Walters, Joanna (2018-10-21). *"#MeToo a revolution that can't be stopped, says Time's Up co-founder"*. the Guardian. Retrieved 2018-10-21.

2. Hemel, Daniel and Lund, Dorothy. Sexual Harassment and Corporate Law. Columbia Law Review. Vol.118 No. 6

3. Rhode, Deborah. How Unusual is the Roger Ailes Sexual Harassment Case. Harvard Business Review. August 10,2016.

4. Stempel, Jonathan. 21st Century Fox in $90 Million Settlement Tied to Sexual Harassment Scandal. Reuters/Entertainment News. November20,2017

CHAPTER 5

PSYCHOLOGICAL PERSPECTIVE

"With integrity, you have nothing to fear,
since you have nothing to hide. With integrity,
you will do the right thing, so you will have no guilt."

—ZIG ZIGLAR

If a company or powerful individual of a company perceives an employee as a potential threat or an actual threat is levied, any power and control available can lead to harassment and ultimately removal of the challenging employee. Judy, an employee of a large company, challenged the behavior and intentions of an executive. The corporate response was extensive and well-resourced. In an effort to protect the identity and security of a powerful employee this challenging worker's identity was instead whittled away. From a qualified, committed, loyal, smart employee, Judy was relegated to the status of a non-essential, undervalued member of the team- no longer needed, no longer esteemed, not wanted. Her credibility and identity went from as she states "hero to zero."

This all begun for Judy in a "business customary" manner. Furthering a work relationship, advancing collegial connections after work, and joining in celebratory drinks have always been common workplace occurrences. Women seek camaraderie and bonding just as much as men do, maybe a little more. Additionally, women have historically augmented their self-definition by who they are in a relationship with- husbands, children, friends, community. Unexpectedly and unfortunately for Judy the "let's connect over a shared victory" became quickly and clearly sexualized when she was referred to as a "lush" and her male counterpart suggesting this could be a regular meeting.

In an attempt to set boundaries and clarify the relationship, Judy initiated discussion of the situation with the executive. Instead of improving the relationship, by voicing her concerns and needs regarding a fellow employee, she set into motion the company and its personnel reevaluating her overall job performance. Her honorable attempt at addressing and processing a work relationship culminated in her losing her work status and finally her own employment.

Specific tactics were used by the company and its employees undermining Judy's performance resulting in her then being judged with poor performance. Position advancement was removed, job description changed and work relationships were altered. She was placed on a performance plan, (which comes with an implicit threat of job security.) She was kept out of meetings (non-inclusion) leaving her less informed and less equipped to manage upcoming requirements and demands of the position. Policy specifics never applied before, were applied to her with no accounting for her overall contribution and work ethic. Workplace studies show "Being ignored, excluded, or overlooked at work inflicts more damage on our physical and mental health than does being harassed."[1]

While working diligently to uphold her self-image and professional conduct Judy was also contending with a quickly growing mistrust. Trusting company personnel personally and professionally, trusting the corporate systems in place, and trusting she could even continue in a corporate world without this retaliation networking its way to other subsequent companies. Originally viewed as a valued, highest level employee gave Judy a sense of protection and job security, apparently a false sense. Marginalized by the individuals who previously granted her high credibility. Judy was in essence redefined as less qualified, less capable, less accomplished. She had gone from a 1 level (top performer) to a 3 level. She was looking in the mirror and seeing a very different reflection from management and peers. Psychologically a newly defined self, even foreign to the individual, results in confusion and some adopting of the imposed attributions and behaviors. Even if the individual's behavior is not influenced, the very act of evaluators *looking* assumes they will "find". Judy was placed in a potentially "gotcha" position. Yet, she overcame the psychological and behavioral tactics and successfully completed her performance plan. Regardless, the company remained the powerful agent, still intent on its own desired outcome. Three weeks later she was fired.

Fortunately, Judy had and has the internal and social resources and psychological wherewithal equipping her to cope and manage this corporate experience and its aftermath. Judy spent most of her adult life networking in numerous contexts. Her self-image and identity developed in the roles she took and contributions she made - socially, within her family, the church and professionally. Judy has a long history of being esteemed, valued, and befriended by many. In turn, her family members, friends and associates offered compassion and understanding in this situation. These internal and external resources upheld Judy's sense of self even though she visited moments of feeling hopeless. Judy's long-held identity and the relationships she developed over the years gave her the needed significant measure of resilience to cope with this professional crisis and continue productively both personally and professionally.

Although Judy's outcome might be unique to her, the corporate intentions and tactics she faced were not. Employees choosing to challenge their company and its workers and culture must be equipped with the lessons, tools and skills - fortified and braced for a difficult challenge with a low rate of survival.

SOURCES

1. Workplace Ostracism More Distressing Than Harassment. Association for Psychological Science. June 13,2014

CHAPTER 6

TIME'S GRASP: THE INTRICACIES OF TIME IN TRAUMATIC WOUNDING

C. Greco

> "What would happen if one woman told the truth about her life?
> The world would split open."
>
> MURIEL RUKEYSER

THE INITIATION

My conversations with Judy began many months ago. Our first meeting reminded me of the numerous prior meetings I had had with women of all ages who needed to speak something of significance that had not as yet been realized. With Judy, and in most cases, I would notice an initial hesitation, a need to apologize for speaking of such horror as well as the concern for my having to listen. For many this would be the first time the words were uttered. It was always painful. These words were the stories that told of objectifications and more. I remember listening to Judy that first time. I was inspired by her courage. Judy, in her willingness to claim what this experience had been for her, pursued a path of self discovery; a questioning of the self so as to deepen in her own understanding and self knowledge. But like many others I had witnessed, what began as self inquiry would veer; would end in an inquisition of the self. A negation of sorts. It carried a weightedness; a heaviness. Upon further investigation, we would find that this negation had been spoken by someone or some system in power in an attempt to avoid accountability for their actions. It had the feel of what is known as gaslighting. Judy's strength served her. Still, like many in the face of circumstances where their integrity (whether that was of bodily integrity, mental integrity, emotional integrity or spiritual) is compromised or denied, internalization of some form of this negation would occur. Once internalized, questions would be query to the very nature of their experience. What was real? Judy's questions took the form of: "Was I too naive?", "Why can't I move on?" and, "Why don't I have another job?" The implication was to assume culpability that was not hers.

I had heard these questions or variations on the theme multiple times. Some were of much stronger self negation. All questions held the elements of denigration, diminution stated or implied by those misusing or abusing their power. The internalization of these elements would give rise to the internal inquisition noted above. As such this would become another burden to be carried. Listening to Judy's words as well as to her tone of voice and watching the language of her body would cue us to this underlying experience. Jointly we would piece together the fragments of remembered experience; the words said, the innuendo, the intonations, the implications, the actions taken. Judy would re-member/remember; would connect the fragments so as to enter into the wholeness of her experience. Time. It was time in connection that would deliver her truth. It was time that would provide trust in her own knowing offering congruence to her life. Questions would be answered. The truth could be acknowledged and lived.

The following is a compilation of learnings from the stories I was privileged to hear. Although my time was mostly spent with women, I know this process to be applicable to all genders.

THE BEGINNING

Some years ago now, my work became focused on time and its relationship to traumatic wounding. Women primarily presented with these issues (Women and children are the most exploited). They carried this burden and sought to understand its lingering; the ongoing impact that continued to haunt their lives. There were similarities and distinctions within each person's experience of the traumatic. Together we began a process of self study that would attend. Time was one of the more universal themes, we discovered. The time it took to address the wound symbolized the amount of devastation that had inevitably occurred within the context. Time, it seemed, would reflect the elements entailed in coming to know the reality of what was; what had been. Integration of any traumatic experience was not possible until one came into her own knowing. This knowing needed to include one's physicality, emotionality and spirituality. Without this integration, life was destined to be incongruent; lived from varied places within the self versus the whole. Through the next few years there would be approximately fifty white women between the ages 30-74 (All had previously been in therapy), who would participate in and define a process that could address what had happened and explore what was needed now for living a life of meaningful connection. Before we could connect and return to life in the world, we would need to establish a relatedness to what had occurred, who we had been, and who we were now in the aftermath. A connection within the interiority of the self needed to take place. Most of us recoiled from this connection due to the residual pain that accompanied it.

My own experience mirrored theirs. Together we would labor to find our way. All of us had spent considerable time on attempts to make sense out of what had happened. Trauma can be seen on a spectrum, not all incidents of trauma the same. (See notes)[2] However, the lasting effects we continued to contend with had qualities resonant to one another. Time and the profound impact on each life were significant. Similarly the cultural response; to move on, get over it, leave the past in the past proved unhelpful. We each understood the ineffectiveness of those words having tried to do this. Later we would understand this as the silencing we had each known. We had found few, if any, willing to speak about this. Few who could apprehend, let alone hear. This added to the separation or alienation that accompanied each experience. The pervasive cultural assumption was that we had done something "wrong" or we were in some way responsible for what had happened. This inordinate victim blaming, contributed to our sense of separation. Forced to live from contradictory realities required energy to maintain. Our shared experience allowed for our expanded study. Though we were small in number, we would bear witness to each other and no longer felt alone.

As we came together to gaze more consciously into the depths of time and the traumatic, we found a gospel reading from Thomas that called to us. We were women of spirit; needed a spiritual base. We began here: Gospel of Thomas; "If you are searching, you must not stop until you find. When you find, however, you will become troubled. Your confusion will give way to wonder. In wonder you will reign over all things. Your sovereignty will be your rest."[3] We had long wrestled within a search; this a search for the real, the truth. Many had resigned themselves to living a life that was not truly theirs. As we engaged together in our quest for more life, hope was renewed. Our search now was for truth, no matter what that truth was. At this juncture in life, it was the truth that mattered. We reasoned that if we had truth, we could live within it, would at least know, would have ground on which to stand. We interpreted the words to the gospel reading as a way to move us into our search with more intentionality. Together, we purported, we could access more hope to face the possibilities of what had been and what it now meant. Our combined energies would serve. We were committed.

Time continued its import and would throughout. Unsure what it was that we could trust, we would, by necessity, return to a past that was fraught with discomfort and horror. Interestingly we had been "returned" many times before but this was now in and of concerted awareness. It was as if we had made the decision to see and to know. Having made this choice, we stepped into the unresolved pain. A counter cultural experience, this was the "...you must not stop until you find..." encounter. Once opened, our eyes would not close. Ambivalence became less accessible. We had no way to know what was ahead, where this would take us. Our sole determination was in knowing the truth. We each searched the truth of our own experience.

The following is written in regard to what we discovered in the hope that it might be useful to those with similar experience. This was a 'together' learning that provided unanticipated knowledge. This the knowledge of the "troubled"ness we engaged in with each expression of the truth and the confusion that gave way to wonder and ultimately to rest. The sovereignty giving us rest would be the trust developed within connection to the self and our lived experience, the truth of who we each were. Time would seemingly, first, constrict, hold us to the traumatic event/s and its pain. Once present, time would befriend/behold us, would school us in beholding. Once learned, time would now inform the present and potential future. Time could then move and move us. We could now go back and forth in time making connections of the past to the present; of the present to a possible future. Connecting to our depths we entered the long avoided suffering we and the culture would have us resist. This deepening connection would allow for our interconnection to the world. Once connected, our isolation lessened. We began to trust in a process we lived into. We trusted in its guidance. Time, as we discovered, was timely. Time offered us what we needed. We could not rush a process that was sacred. Time would offer us new life from the depth of our interconnectedness to the all. Time, thus, became the timeless.

The following includes what we came to know, practices that assisted, and resources we utilized in our self study; our self inquiry.

AN INTRODUCTION TO THE INTRICACIES OF TIME IN TRAUMATIC WOUNDING

As traumatic events occur, they are processed in the mind, body and psyche/spirit in both unique and universal ways. Much has been researched and written with regard to such (See Notes). 4-8 Time is significant in the processing of the traumatic as it can impact all areas of life over the life span. Understanding this, time in the process of attending can serve as well as take. This is difficult for survivors to comprehend while within the context of the event's impact. Since the culture is oft of quick fixes and simple solutions, time spent is seen as unuseful and unproductive. To take time in service to oneself in order to integrate experience is thus denied or seen as unnecessary if one is capable, strong. The culture as a result is unsupportive and often demeaning, adding to the wounding. The culture and many of its members do not want to be bothered. It is presumed that pain is a problem to be denied, that it could have been avoided had one acted in right fashion and so on. Time is then spent in the altering of reality via intellectualizing, spiritualizing, denial, drugs, food, sex or a variety of other means. All in service to that which is unreal.

ALTERATIONS IN TIME

In the initial moments of trauma time is altered. Alterations in time are not completely foreign to human experience. Trauma is defined simply, by the online dictionary,[9] as an extremely disturbing experience and suggests a level of complexity within the body that will engage it in survival. Much of this is outside awareness. The body is skilled in its endeavors to protect life. It is said that the body chooses the best response in the moment. (See notes). 4-8 Because the complexity of the traumatic is too much to comprehend at once, time is altered in service to the whole. Traumatic memory is thus encoded differently. Trauma, taken from the Greek, is literally translated as the "wound"(online dictionary).[9] Time is altered as the event is being internalized; as it is being processed. To survive requires the whole of the body's energy. The amount of time spent in survival may predict the level of difficulty encountered later. Often there is a sense of fragmentation; a split. One acknowledges a before trauma and an after trauma, without a bridge between the two. Ultimately the bridge gets built in elements of time and conscious awareness. Fragmentation is trauma's code.

Within the alterations of time and the fragmentation produced by traumatic experience, one is left disconnected within the self. There may be a sense that something is missing. Gaps in memory exist or memory may be separated from emotion. Time's usual chronology is absent. Time is either slow moving or ceases to move while one's outer life goes on. Dissociation may occur. One may find herself on the ceiling witnessing the event from above, or the experience may have the quality of feeling unreal. Pieces of time in the event may be acutely and accurately remembered while other components not at all. Therefore, questions can remain for years. Life as it was known, however, ceases to exist.

Still survivors want to resume their lives. As they attempt to do so there is some need to both re-member/remember and to not. Those surrounding the survivor tend to be equally conflicted. As such there is little support to access further memory or consciously return to the event. However, because of the encoding of traumatic memory, the memory remains housed within the body. Often the event and its wounding are put aside until later in life. Over months, even years, the appearance of living a "functional" and even a life of high achievement may be displayed. At some crucial point in one's life, however, access is given and the woundedness becomes apparent. Frequently, it becomes apparent through time distortions.

DISTORTIONS IN TIME

Distortions in time may go unrecognized for long periods. As fragmentation continues, the pieces are often compartmentalized so that they remain dismembered, or disconnected from each other and the whole. Distortions in time arise in many ways, from flashbacks to triggers to sleep disturbance, and more. Frequently distortions are recognized in excessive emotion unwarranted for a particular situation. Essentially this is the way in which the past invades the present. It was at this point that we, as women in search, entered into connection with one another. Noticing as the past arose in the present was disconcerting, but it did garner the need for our quest together; our search for the truth. Sometimes it was a fragment of memory that surfaced in a moment being lived. It could be jarring. It might be an emotion that was suddenly available yet seemingly unconnected to the present. Often it would be a body sensation; a smell; a quiver in the arms or legs out of proportion for the situation being lived. Suffice it to say that it was both strong enough and discordant enough so as to call us to attention. It would happen more than once. It would not let up. It would not let go.

Time seemed split; distorted in that the past existed in the now. Eventually these distortions required that we take notice in order to make sense out of what was occurring. Frequently it was frightening. It could feel as though a past horror was being lived through. We had little control over its bodily presence or when that past endeavor would show up to claim us. It could happen anywhere at any time. With every occurrence weathered, we would believe it was now over; done. Instead, it persisted. We could not alter it within the mind; no way to think our way out. We could not spiritualize it either. Once the "door" had opened, fragments of past were accessible but not in any order. The initial step was to begin to recognize where we were in time and space. Time would now seemingly hold us to past terrors unresolved but long put away. In this way it was as though time constricted around these events. The past became present. We were not initially, welcoming.

TIME CONSTRICTS

Acknowledging where we were in time and space suggested to us an embodiment of sorts. Since one of the strategies for survival had been to leave the body via dissociating, intellectualizing or spiritualizing, we recognized that the body had information for us the mind could not provide. (See notes). 4-8 This was apparent when the past arrived in the present in the form of physical sensations. These examples were: the breath would become shallow, the heart might race, nausea would present and so on. It was as though we needed to learn a new language, this the language of the body. Each of us would need to decipher our own body's cues. Seeking our "ground" we sat on the floor when we gathered. We established a sense of the physical, the body as grounding us in the present, a container of sorts, and our physicality as our potential guidance. In this way we honed our effectiveness in engaging somatic experience.

The process was problematic in that it seemingly required time we did not think we had. We had to work, had families that needed attending. Still, whether we took the time to be aware or not, the past continued its presence. At some point, we realized that it took more energy to avoid or resist the past than to allow for its communication. Non-resistance became our way of being with. We began to work with the concept of witnessing. Mostly, though, we wanted it over. We wanted to be done. Time constricted; time contracted around what had been traumatic. For some, this trauma might have been a single event, but for many it was a number of events, or as in the case of domestic violence or developmental trauma, it had taken place over a period of time.

Returning to our spiritual base and the Gospel of Thomas quote, "…you must search until you find…," we carried on in some quandary and with questions. We now looked for the stabilization of our ground; the "…ground of our being…" [10], which for us meant a sense of the spiritual within the context of matter; the physical presence of the body. We would learn that with each fragment of memory we accessed, connection could be made within the integral of mind/body/spirit. This would ultimately provide for integration and an ability to live from the whole of our beings. Many complained of the slow pace this required. Later we would know it as foundational. At some point we discerned that time was no longer constricting, but now "held" us as though pensive, contemplative, unknowing. And we, entered here.

TIME HOLDS

Being held by time was a bit of comfort. It allowed for the sense of possibility that had not occurred to us before since much energy had been utilized in trying to keep ourselves safe. What came next, however, was anguish, the recognition that once we knew our ground, we had access to emotion that had been previously hindered in its expression. Often these feeling states would be triggered in our day-to- day life experience only now with such vigor, we would struggle to contain them. This would require our learning to delineate, once again, time frames that might be in competition for declaration. It demanded our need for bearing witness. What was past might need different expression versus what we were called to express in the moment at work, with friends or family. Compulsions to speak, did not serve.

Aurora Levins Morales notes:

"...what is so dreadful is that to transform the traumatic we must re-enter it fully, and allow the full weight of grief to pass through our hearts. It is not possible to digest atrocity without tasting it first, without assessing on our tongues the full bitterness of it. Our society does not do grief well or easily, and what is required to face trauma is the ability to mourn, fully and deeply, all that has been taken from us"

(MORALES, P.19). [11]

We would begin now, to learn distinctions between keeping secret and holding sacred. Practices of containment, acknowledging the energetics of emotion while letting the energy accumulate in the body, so as to speak from the "ground" of one's being was complex learning. There would be many mistakes as we grew into this implementation. Journaling would prove to be of great assistance as would body movement and breath awareness. All of these added to the possibility of integration. We would call our work together, "Engendering Warmth." These words inspired by the writings of Clarissa Pinkola Estes in her work, *Women Who Run With The Wolves* [12]. Our sense of our spirituality now interwoven with our phys-icality and our humanity, our feeling states now called to us for further instruction. With this would arise invasions of thought, of old patterns, and beliefs we had held in order to survive. Now, as in accordance with the gospel reading; we would become troubled.

Paying attention to emotional content, we learned, was not to be disavowed, but like the body, offered us information of importance. Our feeling states were not literal truth to be lived from but sites of data to be discovered. The diversity of this experience offered once again its beauty and its complexity. Each of us had to learn yet another deciphering of trauma's cues. We also came to know that each feeling state had a bodily sensation that offered detail that might accommodate our learning. Now time would befriend us. In its befriending, the past would inform the present.

TIME BEFRIENDS

We were troubled, but also able to trust more in the process. Coming to speech we were returned to early years, to growing up, to remembrances of long ago. Beginning to speak, grounded in our physicality, our humanity, and informed by feeling states, we now accessed memory of the incidents long past and long forgotten where our speech had been tampered with; where our voices had been denied. Suddenly conscious of memories of silencing; of the negation of voice, we explored what had been. Looking out from the depths we had engaged, we saw from the past and into the culture; the world at large. Here we encountered the inequities of power, their role in our silencing, their role in the perpetuation of untruth. Grief now made a grand entrance.

Confusion would accompany the grief. As we looked out and into the world, we embarked on a journey that connected the past to the present. Tarana Burke and the #MeToo Movement in its early years made its way into our minds/hearts. Moving between grief and confusion, time continued to befriend and would allow for the deepening connectivity within the soul and the presence of the degradation, diminution, and dehumanization we had endured at the hands of those in power. We realized how much time had been spent in self blame; in trying to make sense out of the whys of traumatic experience.

In the words of Aurora Levins Morales:

"Whether it takes place in the supposedly private context of sexual abuse or the public and allegedly impersonal arenas of colonialism, patriarchy or a profoundly racist class society, the traumatic experience of being dehumanized and exploited strips people of their stories, of the explanations that make sense in their lives. Instead, it imposes on us the self-justifying mythologies of the perpetrators. We are left adrift, the connection between cause and effect severed so that we are unable to identify the sources of our pain."

13

Time in the truth was returning to us our stories. The truth was, however, unfathomable and in some ways, worse than we had expected. Recognizing that the self blame we had engaged in was a survival strategy; the surmising that if we could "fix" what was wrong with us we would have more control and might then live into a better life. This we now knew to be subterfuge. To learn that the truth was we had been powerlessness in the face of those who would misuse; abuse their power, was incomprehensible; unbearable. Yet, this was the story of our lived experience. Our long imposed isolation had been based in strategies developed to survive and had been in collusion with a culture that suggested our culpability. This truth now opened us to our interrelatedness as women on this journey. Out of our deepest grief, our woundedness, and out of our suffering would arise a deepening connectedness to each other and to all afflicted. No longer separate or uncommon, we were part of the larger whole. We would come to know this as time's beholding.

Judith Herman notes:

> In order to escape accountability for his crimes, the perpetrator does everything in his power to promote forgetting. Secrecy and silence are the perpetrator's first line of defense. If secrecy fails, the perpetrator attacks the credibility of his victim. If he cannot silence her absolutely, he tries to make sure no-one listens. To this end, he marshals an impressive array of arguments, from the most blatant denial to the most sophisticated and elegant rationalization. After every atrocity one can expect to hear the same predictable apologies: it never happened; the victim lies; the victim exaggerates; the victim brought it on herself; and in any case it is time to forget the past and move on. The more powerful the perpetrator, the greater his prerogative to name and define reality, and the more completely his arguments prevail.
>
> [14]

TIME BEHOLDS

In attending to our grief, we began to "stand." This allowed us to engage a stance of truth that would reflect the story of each of our lives. This would be a literal stance of the body; the body in connection to the mind and spirit. Untruths now visible, we could decline them. The survival stories of the old, having once saved us now disturbed us physically, emotionally and spiritually. Their falseness supported by the culture added further dimension to our grief.

Judith Herman notes:

> "The perpetrator's arguments prove irresistible when the bystander
> faces them in isolation. Without a supportive social environment, the
> bystander usually succumbs to the temptation to look the other way.
> This is true even when the victim is a valued member of society...
> when the victim is already devalued (a woman, a child), she may find
> that the most traumatic events of her life take place outside the realm
> of socially validated reality. Her experience becomes unspeakable".
>
> 15

Our perceived isolation now made sense as we sought to "unlearn" while trusting in the authenticity of our experience.

Removal of perceived culpability allowed us energy to breathe deeply and to "be" more of who we were. The beginnings of truth assimilated allowed for the possibility of an integrated life; only a glimpse in time but a glimpse of profound relevance for each of us. Re-memberings now were a source of our becoming. We would engage in truth telling; the truth of the stories we had lived, the truth emerging out of the silence we had held, and the truth we would now claim and live into. The quote by Muriel Rukeyser (above) called to us.

Living into the story that was ours, re-membering; putting the pieces together, we were delivered a sense of the integral self; a re-membered/remembered self. This was the self who had survived. This, the beginnings of the sacredness of an integrated life. This a life of connectedness, of meaning and of integrity. Through integration we would know the "feel" of truth in the body, a guiding knowledge to living authentically; the beholding of the self and a living from the inside out. Through integration we would recognize a sense of our embodied presence; who we had been throughout and who we were. It was from this place that we would speak, tell the truth of our lives; the resonance of truth within the voice we now claimed as our own. "Confusion" was giving way. Time could now open.

TIME OPENS

Aware now of our own embodied presence we had access, openings to memories of great pleasure; sacred moments of times past. Our experience becoming more of the both/and, versus the either/or. Blame of self, blame of others ceased. Words and the premise of those words shifted. We spoke now of responsibility; of account-ability. The feel of truth in the body guided us. The integral ground of our being; the honor of life lived in the consciousness of our integrity, returned us to memories of childlike wonder. Albeit brief at the outset, these memories would serve as a glimpse of a possible future that could embrace the whole of life. No longer defined or held by the traumatic, our entrance into more fullness governed and elicited a broader consciousness. There would be no forgetting. There would be no closure. Only space for more and more life.

As time passed, we were increasingly able to access this sense of self, the embodiment of our presence, this the essence of who we were; giving meaning to life. To know our own sense of presence and to live from that presence would further determine our choices, our actions. We would live an informed life, a life of inclusivity, of equity of presence. Having been granted the ability to "see" backward and forward in time, we could acknowledge time as infinitely more fluid than we had known. Opening time allowed for continued learning. Literal and linear were unwelcome guests, but served to call for more space in our being, in our becoming.

Returning to the Gospel of Thomas, we came to understand that embodied and integral presence offered us a sense of personal power, the power to choose responses of integrity in the moment. This the power to co-create life as life is lived. Integration would be an ongoing process we would commit to throughout life. This the sustained desire for engaging in more life through its continual instruction. The power of self knowledge, its offering of wisdom.

This a very distinct form of power, used only as power with, or "reign;" not reign over, but reign with. Time now verged on the mystical, a becoming of the timeless. And a place we might rest assured in the never ending remembered story that would call us to our own ongoing becoming.

TIMELESS

Committed to the process of our integration and the re-membrance of the Self which included re-memberings of the objectification, the degradation, the dehumanization, the diminution we had each experienced; the bridge between our "before" and "after" was built. Having spent years acknowledging loss, wishing "this" hadn't happened, wishing that we could return to life as it had been; we now entered into our own lives as they were, as they had come to be. Once the fragments of memory were integrated, we could piece together the whole of our lives. Grief accompanied each fragment and within the process of integrating, access was gained to a greater sense of the self. Being re-membered, life now made sense. Life's meaning was nurtured. We could cross the bridge again and again, returning to memories of the all of life. We had the freedom to choose to remember. Time had no need to constrict. Here, on the bridge, we met the fullness of time. Our consciousness was opened.

This experience of the "timeless" connected us to those who had gone before us, those who had contributed to this path. Our ancestors and the collective wisdom of the past moving us toward a future we could live into, become part of. Being re-membered was an inclusive experience, honored the whole of life; the suffering, the joy. Having lived into and through our pain, we now had access to the world's pain. The deepening connection to the self, strengthening our connection to the all. Here we engaged in the reverence of all life. This reverence furthered our becoming. That which was timeless served the reality of what was, not pretense but truth. Our search for truth now bearing fruit, the fruit of our broadening consciousness. We could now understand. We could live. We could be.

The "wonder" from the Gospel of Thomas quote, we now lived into and through. This gift of our integration providing the nature of presence we could assume. Through integration our integrity would be restored. Our dignity would reign. The timelessness of being and the animating of our consciousness would render our significance. The world appeared different, yet familiar. The work was and continued to be of great diligence. Our choices were now of increased clarity, of embodied integrity and were also inherently complex. We would find within ourselves abilities to hear and to see in new ways that would offer increased information on many levels. Time would continue its revelations. And as noted by Clarissa Pinkola Estes, "...we (understood) understand that it is now our work for life." [16]

In hindsight we would recognize that time had taken us, held us, would behold us, would provide us our sovereignty, and ultimately would give us to ourselves. In the claiming of each story, its offering of truth; we would deliver truth to the world.

SOURCES

1. Scaer, Robert. The Trauma Spectrum. W.W. Norton & Company Inc.: New York, 2005.

2. Bourgeault, Cynthia. The Wisdom Way of Knowing; the Gospel of Thomas, Logion 2.

3. Berceli, David. Trauma Release Exercises. BookSurge Publishing, North Charleston, SC, 2005.

4. Levine, Peter. Waking the Tiger. North Atlantic Books, Berkeley, CA, 1997.

5. Miller, Alice. The Body Never Lies. W.W. Norton & Company Inc.: New York, 2005.

6. Porges, Stephen. The Polyvagal Theory. W.W. Norton & Company Inc.: New York, 2011.

7. Van der Kolk, Bessel. The Body Keeps the Score. Penguin Publishing Group: London (?)2014.

8. Online dictionary

9. Emmet, Dorothy. "'THE GROUND OF BEING'." The Journal of Theological Studies, vol 15, no. 2, 1964, pp. 280-292. JSTOR, www.jstor.org/stable/23953940.

10. Levins Morales, Aurora. Medicine Stories. South End Press: Cambridge, MA,1998.

11. Estes, Clarissa Pinkola. Women who Run with the Wolves. Ballantine Books, NY 1992.

12. Levins Morales, p. 2-3

13. Herman, Judith Lewis. Trauma and Recovery. Basic Books, New York, NY 1992.

14. Herman, Judith Lewis. P. 8

15. Rukeyser, Muriel. The Collected Poems of Muriel Rukeyser. University of Pittsburgh Press, 2006.

16. Estes, Clarissa Pinkola Estes, p. 384

CHAPTER 7

LEGAL: HARASSMENT IN THE WORKPLACE—ARE THERE LEGAL REMEDIES?

"Any action that is dictated by fear or by coercion of any kind ceases to be moral."

—Mohandas Gandhi

There is little doubt in 2019 that harassment in the work place (including but not limited to harassment on the basis of sex, race, religion and national origin) is still a major issue for employees and employers. Liability can attach not just to the company but in some limited instances can include individuals who are managers or even corporate directors who are aware of harassment and fail to take appropriate steps to address the issue. Individual liability is very difficult to establish, however, so it is not a significant factor when considering ways to deal with the continuing phenomenon of harassment. Therefore, despite laws prohibiting harassment that have been on the books for some 50 years, harassment and discrimination continue. Harassment and discrimination require proof of intent in most instances. The victim must prove that the company's agents were motivated to harass an individual because of race, sex, age or one of the other limited areas covered by the law. It is difficult to prove intent if the company's agents are able to hide the real motives at play.

Some believe that because intent is at the heart of proving a legal case, harassment has become more subtle and hidden in the workplace in order to protect harassers. There is a lot of truth to that assertion. Employers and managers in many large firms are certainly aware that outright express or direct harassment will bring down the wrath of the HR department and could result in trouble for the harasser. They often have been required to attend programs about harassment in the workplace and they learn what can create legal liability. Some commentators believe that effectively, we have trained managers how to avoid liability for harassment, not how to prevent harassment.

Today, more subtle forms of harassment tend to dominate the corporate environment. Judy's story is a good example of that scenario. She experiences an inappropriate advance from a manager. She tries to set boundaries and deal with the matter on her own. But challenging the authority of her managers brought her from hero to zero through forms of more subtle harassment and discrimination. The individuals involved denied any ill motive, as usual. But the circumstances speak for themselves. She is downgraded, excluded, ostracized, and her life at work becomes a living nightmare. When she asks to leave, the HR response is to pretend there is nothing wrong—why would we give you a package when you are a good performer? You just need to work through your issues because it is your problem and not ours. Once she has spoken out, however, she is doomed. No one listens to her or tries to understand what is happening to her. Real motives are hidden behind a web of lies, cover-ups, and repressive behavior designed to humiliate and retaliate.

When Judy realizes she is not going to be listened to by HR and the managers, she seeks legal help. The result? In effect, she has wasted her time. Why? Because the legal standards demand specific forms of evidence—concrete examples of harassment such as statements of ill motive on the part of her managers. She has to prove intent. Smartly, her employer did not take overt steps to fire her, which again, would have helped Judy's legal case. Instead, they waited her out while they took steps to subtly change her work and ensure she did not have access to high profile work. She was supposed to be happy with her situation, so she is told. They also smartly removed her from direct contact with the manager who initiated the inappropriate conduct; again, this limited Judy's legal claims. And they played for time. They could wait her out.

Many persons in Judy's situation find little solace in the legal system because it is so difficult to prove intent which is at the heart of the law, from indirect, subtle forms of harassment. It is her word against his and the company, and when the actions are subtle or the specific inappropriate conduct is denied, the case is difficult to prove.

While not necessarily evident in Judy's case, another form of harassment that is frequently sited is bullying. The workplace bully, if a manager, can make life miserable for an employee. But proving discriminatory intent on the part of the workplace bully is difficult when this person bullies others as well. The term 'equal opportunity harasser' is used to describe this person and in part, to deny any ill motive as everyone is treated poorly and thus, liability cannot be established as the law is interpreted.

Another difficulty with the current legal system is the inability to address anonymous allegations of harassment. Anonymous harassers are often frowned upon because they won't come forward directly but they make allegations that can possibly ruin a reputation if the allegations are false. But look what happens when you step forward like Judy did—nothing helped her situation. Her reputation was ruined. Employers under the law have an obligation to review any possible situation where harassment is alleged—but as long as they take some effective response to the allegation, they might avoid liability even if harassment did occur. Anonymous harassers in some unique situations can help stop harassment, usually if the allegations are later supported by many others when the company reviews the allegations. However, one on one allegations of harassment generally are not handled well when reported anonymously. And as in Judy's case, her word against his means she likely is going to be unable to make a claim.

The frustration with the legal system's inability to make much of a dent in harassment may have helped contribute to two recent observations. First, the "me too" movement is to some extent a manifestation of the frustration with failure to address harassment. But the typical individual cannot attract media attention to a harassment allegation. More people like Judy might come forward in the workplace, but that does not mean the workplace is ready to accept these allegations let alone, give them any credit. She contacted the head of the company to no avail, apparently. Judy could not get headlines so no need to worry about her.

Unabated harassment has also become increasingly recognized as a shortcoming in the culture of a business. A recent study by two members of the EEOC concluded that nothing can be done to change the harassment culture unless a corporation and its employees fully embrace a desire to have a workplace that does not tolerate harassment, bullying or any similar conduct. Laws and regulations can only do so much, as is clearly evident in this story. The real battleground is with human resources, corporate management and corporate boards. Are they willing to establish a workplace that allows everyone to bring their entire selves to work each day without fear of reprisal, harassment or bullying? It is about individuals and companies making the commitment to change their culture. This is the best way to decrease the impact of harassment in the workplace. Judy's story is one that can help those who don't experience harassment, to understand how serious this issue remains in our workplace today. If you were running a company, who do you want as managers? Do you want them making inappropriate advances to employees? Do you want to support coverups? Do you want to drive away good employees? Do you stand for fair and impartial investigations? Only senior management and corporate boards can drive the culture necessary to stop situations like this.

CHAPTER 8

EQUAL EMPLOYMENT OPPORTUNITY COMMISSION (EEOC) SELECT TASK FORCE ON THE STUDY OF HARASSMENT IN THE WORK FORCE: EXECUTIVE SUMMARY, KEY STATISTICS, AND THE CASE OF THE "SUPERSTAR" HARASSER

"One by one, women who had lived in silence about their own experiences of sexual harassment and assault — whether due to negative career repercussions, fear of not being believed, shame, NDAs, and other reasons — began to **share their stories**, adding voices to a booming chorus under the hashtag **#MeToo**. They demanded that widespread behavior of intimidation and abuse of power, and the normalization of it, come to an end."

—Article ME TOO OCT. 19, 2017,
25 Famous Women on Sexual Harassment and Assault
By Julie Ma

This information is quoted from the EEOC: Study of Harassment in the Work Force a Report of Co-Chairs Chai R. Feldblum & Victoria A. Lipnic: Executive Summary & Recommendations (June 2016)

Thirty years ago, the US Supreme Court recognized claims for sexual harassment as a form of discrimination based on sex under Title VII of the Civil Rights Act of 1964. Six years Chai R. Vellum and Victoria A. Lipnic came to the EEOC in 2000 and were struck by how many cases sexual harassment the EEOC continues to deal with every year. They established a Select Task Force on the Study of Harassment in the Workplace. This Select Task Force consisted of experts in management, plaintiff's attorneys, employer advocacy groups, labor representatives, academics who have studied this field for years-sociologists, psychologists, and experts in organizational behavior. The group was heavy on lawyers, the approach considered the social science on harassment in the workplace. Also witnesses participated in 8 meetings. The study was initiated in January 2015 and completed in June 2016 which was completed over 18 months.

Workplace Harassment Remains a Persistent Problem. Almost fully one third of the approximately 90,000 charges received by EEOC in fiscal year 2015 included an allegation of workplace harassment. This includes, among other things, charges of unlawful harassment on the basis of sex (including sexual orientation, gender identity, and pregnancy), race, disability, age, ethnicity/national origin, color, and religion. While there is robust data and academic literature on sex-based harassment, there is very limited data regarding harassment on other protected bases. More research is needed.

Workplace Harassment Too Often Goes Unreported. Common workplace-based responses by those who experience sex-based harassment are to avoid the harasser, deny or downplay the gravity of the situation, or attempt to ignore, forget, or endure the behavior. The least common response to harassment is to take some formal action – either to report the harassment internally or file a formal legal complaint. Roughly *three out of four* individuals who experienced harassment never even talked to a supervisor, manager, or union representative about the harassing conduct. Employees who experience harassment fail to report the harassing behavior or to file a complaint because they fear disbelief of their claim, inaction on their claim, blame, or social or professional retaliation.

There Is a Compelling Business Case for Stopping and Preventing Harassment. When employers consider the costs of workplace harassment, they often focus on legal costs, and with good reason. Last year, EEOC alone recovered $164.5 million for workers alleging harassment –and these direct costs are just the tip of the iceberg. *Workplace harassment first and foremost comes at a steep cost to those who suffer it, as they experience mental, physical, and economic harm. Beyond that, workplace harassment affects all workers, and its true cost includes decreased productivity, increased turnover, and reputational harm for the company. All of this is a drag on performance – and the bottom-line.*

It Starts at the Top – Leadership and Accountability Are Critical. Workplace culture has the greatest impact on allowing harassment to flourish, or conversely, in preventing harassment. The importance of leadership cannot be overstated – effective harassment prevention efforts, and workplace culture in which harassment is not tolerated, must start with and involve the highest level of management of the company. But a commitment (even from the top) to a diverse, inclusive, and respectful workplace is not enough. Rather, at all levels, across all positions, an organization must have systems in place that hold employees accountable for this expectation. Accountability systems must ensure that those who engage in harassment are held responsible in a meaningful, appropriate, and proportional manner, and that those whose job it is to prevent or respond to harassment should be rewarded for doing that job well (or penalized for failing to do so). Finally, leadership means ensuring that anti-harassment efforts are given the necessary time and resources to be effective.

Training Must Change. Much of the training done over the last 30 years has not worked as a prevention tool – it's been too focused on simply avoiding legal liability. We believe effective training can reduce workplace harassment, and recognize that ineffective training can be unhelpful or even counterproductive. However, even effective training cannot occur in a vacuum – it must be part of a holistic culture of non-harassment that starts at the top. Similarly, one size does *not* fit all: Training is most effective when tailored to the specific workforce and workplace, and to different cohorts of employees. Finally, when trained correctly, middle-managers and first-line supervisors in particular can be an employer's most valuable resource in preventing and stopping harassment.

New and Different Approaches to Training Should Be Explored. We heard of several new models of training that may show promise for harassment training. "Bystander intervention training" – increasingly used to combat sexual violence on school campuses – empowers co-workers and gives them the tools to intervene when they witness harassing behavior, and show promise for harassment prevention. Workplace "civility training" that does not focus on eliminating unwelcome or offensive behavior based on characteristics protected under employment non-discrimination laws, but rather on promoting respect and civility in the workplace generally, likewise may offer solutions.

It's On Us. Harassment in the workplace will not stop on its own – it's on all of us to be part of the fight to stop workplace harassment. We cannot be complacent bystanders and expect our workplace cultures to change themselves. For this reason, we suggest exploring the launch of an *It's on Us* campaign for the workplace. Originally developed to reduce sexual violence in educational settings, the *It's on Us* campaign is premised on the idea that students, faculty, and campus staff should be empowered to be part of the solution to sexual assault, and should be provided the tools and resources to prevent sexual assault as engaged bystanders. Launching a similar *It's on Us* campaign in workplaces across the nation – large and small, urban and rural – is an audacious goal. But doing so could transform the problem of workplace harassment from being about targets, harassers, and legal compliance, into one in which co-workers, supervisors, clients, and customers all have roles to play in stopping such harassment.

The final report also includes detailed recommendations and a number of helpful tools to aid in designing effective anti-harassment policies; developing training curricula; implementing complaint, reporting, and investigation procedures; creating an organizational culture in which harassment is not tolerated; ensuring employees are held accountable; and assessing and responding to workplace "risk factors" for harassment

KEY STATISTICS SHARED

In FY2015, the *EEOC* received over 28,000 harassment claims for both private and public employers (e.g. government). This is almost a full third of the approximately 90,000 charges of employment discrimination received in 2015.Of the total number of charges received in FY2015 that alleged harassment from employees working for private employers or for state and local government employers, approximately:

- 45% alleged harassment on the basis of sex,

- 34% alleged harassment on the basis of race,

- 19% alleged harassment on the basis of disability,

- 15% alleged harassment on the basis of age,

- 13% alleged harassment on the basis of national origin, and

- 5% alleged harassment on the basis of religion.[11]

Of the total number of complaints filed in FY2015 by federal employees alleging harassment approximately:

- 44% alleged harassment on the basis of sex

- 36% alleged harassment on the basis of race,

- 34% alleged harassment on the basis of disability,

- 26% alleged harassment on the basis of age,

- 12% alleged harassment on the basis of national origin, and

- 5% alleged harassment on the basis of religion

- The numbers of charges (in the private sector) and complaints (in the federal sector) that were filed in FY2015 provide a snapshot of the number of people who sought a formal process to complain about harassment that year.

- Conversely, the number is presumably under-inclusive because *approximately 90% of individuals who say they have experienced harassment never take formal action against the harassment, such as filing a charge or a complaint.*

    - In terms of filing a formal complaint, the percentages tend to be quite low. *Studies have found that 6% to 13% of individuals who experience harassment file a formal complaint. That means, on average, anywhere from 87% to 94% of individuals did not file a formal complaint.*

    - Employees who experience harassment fail to report the behavior or to file a complaint because they anticipate and fear a number of reactions-disbelief of their claim, inaction on their claim, receipt of blame for causing the offending actions; social retaliation (including humiliation and ostracism); and professional retaliation, such as damage to their career and reputation.

- The fears that stop most employees from reporting harassment are well founded. *One 2003 Study found that 75% of employees who spoke out against workplace mistreatment faced some form of retaliation.*

- Other studies have found that sexual harassment reporting is often followed by organizational indifference or trivialization of the harassment complaint as well as reprisals against the victim.

- Such responses understandably harm the victim in terms of adverse job repercussions and psychological distress. These findings raise serious concerns.

- Based on testimony to the Select Task Force and academic articles, they learned anywhere from 25% to 85% of women report having experienced sexual harassment in the workplace. The study refers to different types of surveys. The difference in the range of percentages comes from differences in types of sampling and how respondents and/or researchers define the term sexual harassment.

- Most of the surveys of sex-based harassment at work have focused on harassment experienced by women.

- One exception has been the surveys conducted by the Merit Systems Protection Board of federal employees in 1980, 1987, and 1994. When respondents were asked whether they had experienced unwanted sexual attention or sexual coercion, 42% of women and 15% of men responded in the affirmative in 1981; as did 42% of women and 14% of men in 1988; and 44% of women and 19% of men in 1994.

THE CASE OF THE "SUPERSTAR" HARASSER

Finally, an often competing economic consideration bears discussion. Employers may find themselves in a position where the harasser is a workplace "superstar."[112] By superstar, think of the high-earning trader at an investment bank, the law firm partner who brings in lucrative clients, or the renowned professor or surgeon.[113] Some of these individuals, as with any employee, may be as likely to engage in harassment as others. Often, however, superstars are privileged with higher income, better accommodations, and different expectations.[114] That privilege can lead to a self-view that they are above the rules, which can foster mistreatment.[115] Psychologists have detailed how power can make an individual feel uninhibited and thus more likely to engage in inappropriate behaviors.[116] In short, superstar status can be a breeding ground for harassment.

When the superstar misbehaves, employers may perceive themselves in a quandary. They may be tempted to ignore the misconduct because, the thinking goes, losing the superstar would be too costly. They may wager that the likelihood or cost of a complaint of misbehavior is relatively low and outweighed by the superstar's productivity. Some employers may even use this type of rationale to cover or retaliate for a harasser.

Employers should avoid the trap of binary thinking that weighs the productivity of a harasser *solely* against the costs of his or her being reported. As a recent Harvard Business School study found, the profit consequences of so-called "toxic workers" – *specifically including* those who are "top performers" – is a net negative.[117] Analyzing data on 11 global companies and 58,542 hourly workers, the researchers found that roughly one in 20 workers was fired for egregious company policy violations, such as sexual harassment.[118] Avoiding these toxic workers, they found, can save a company more than twice as much as the increased output generated by a top performer.[119] As a result, the study urged employers to "consider toxic and productivity outcomes together rather than relying on productivity alone as the criterion of a good hire."[120] No matter who the harasser is, the negative effects of harassment can cause serious damage to a business. Indeed, the reputational costs alone can have serious consequences, particularly where it is revealed that managers for years "looked the other way" at a so-called "superstar" harasser.[121]

SOURCES

The numbers in the paragraph above refer to where information was sited from in the study.

Documentation came from: Feldblum, Chai and Lipnic, Victoria. Select Task Force on the Study of Harassment in the Workplace: Executive Summary and Recommendations. June, 2016.

Please refer to the EEOC study for additional information , study includes footnotes to highlight where studies and statistical data came from plus tools to help address sexual harassment in the work force: *https://www.eeoc.gov/eeoc/task_force/harassment/report_summary.cfm*

If you or someone you know wishes to file a sexual harassment claim through the EEOC, please visit *https://www.eeoc.gov/laws/types/sexual_harassment.cfm* for more information. Consult your company's sexual harassment policy to file a sexual harassment complaint through your work, as well.

CHAPTER 9

EEOC BEST PRACTICES, CHECK LISTS AND CHART OF RISK FACTORS TO ELIMINATE HARASSMENT IN THE WORKPLACE

"Innovation and best practices can be sown throughout an organization - but only when they fall on fertile ground."

—Marcus Buckingham

BEST PRACTICES FOR EMPLOYERS

RECOMMENDATIONS FOR LEADERSHIP ACCOUNTABILITY

- A culture where harassment is not tolerated, and in which respect and civility are promoted.

- Assess for risk factors for harassment and minimize risks.

- Conduct climate surveys to assess the extent to which harassment is a problem within your organization.

- Ensure that the company has sufficient resources for harassment prevention efforts

    - Ensure policies and efforts by organization are effective.

    - Reinforce leaderships commitment to creating a workplace free of harassment.

- Ensure when harassment is found to have occurred prompt and proportionate to the severity, discipline is consistent, and does not give undue favor to a particular employee.

- Mid-level managers and frontline supervisors are accountable for preventing and/or responding to harassment.

    - Include the use of metrics and performance review.

- Include in your diversity and inclusion strategy and budget, harassment prevention should be an integral part of the strategy.

RECOMMENDATIONS FOR HARASSMENT PREVENTION POLICIES AND PROCEDURES

- Adopt and maintain a comprehensive anti-harassment policy (which prohibits harassment and includes social media considerations)

- Within the Anti-Harassment Policy, a procedure should be defined for complaints and how to report observed harassment.

- Reporting procedures that are multifaceted, offer a range of methods, multiple points of contact, and geographic and organizational diversity where possible, for employee to report harassment.

- Employers should be alert for any possibility of retaliation against an employee who reports harassment and should take steps to ensure that retaliation does not occur.

- Periodically "test" their reporting system to determine how well the system is working.

- Devote sufficient resources so that workplace investigations are prompt, objective, and thorough. Investigations should be kept as confidential as possible and anonymity will not always be attainable.

- Employers should ensure that where harassment is found to have occurred, discipline is prompt and proportionate to the behavior(s) at issue and the severity of the infraction. Employers should ensure that discipline is consistent, and does not give (or create the appearance of) undue favor to any particular employee.

- In unionized workplaces, the labor union should ensure that its own policy and reporting system meet the principles outlined in this section.

- Groups of employers should consider coming together to offer researchers access to their workplaces to research the effectiveness of their policies, reporting systems, investigative procedures, and corrective actions put into place by those employers, in a manner that would allow research data to be aggregated in a manner that would not identify individual employers.

RECOMMENDATIONS REGARDING ANTI-HARASSMENT COMPLIANCE TRAINING

- Employers should offer, on a regular basis and in a universal manner, compliance trainings that include the content and follow the structural principles described in this report, and which are offered on a dynamic and repeated basis to all employees.

- Employers should dedicate sufficient resources to train middle-management and first-line supervisors on how to respond effectively to harassment that they observe, that is reported to them, or of which they have knowledge or information – even before such harassment reaches a legally-actionable level.

- EEOC should, as a best practice in cases alleging harassment, seek as a condition of its settlement agreements, conciliation agreements, and consent decrees, an agreement that researchers will be allowed to work with the employer to assess the climate and level of harassment in respondent workplaces pre- and post-implementation of compliance trainings, and to study the impact and efficacy of specific training components. Where possible, this research should focus not only on the efficacy of training in large organizations, but also smaller employers and newer or "start up" firms. While we encourage EEOC to seek such an agreement when appropriate, we do not suggest that the agency must do so in all instances, or that failure to obtain such an agreement should derail otherwise acceptable settlement proposals.

- Groups of employers should consider coming together to offer researchers access to their workplaces to research the effectiveness of trainings, particularly in the context of holistic harassment prevention efforts, in a manner that would allow research data to be aggregated and not identify individual employers.

RECOMMENDATIONS REGARDING WORKPLACE CIVILITY AND BYSTANDER INTERVENTION TRAINING

- Employers should consider including workplace civility training and bystander intervention training as part of a holistic harassment prevention program.

- Researchers should assess the impact of workplace civility training on reducing the level of harassment in the workplace.

RECOMMENDATIONS REGARDING TARGETED OUTREACH TO YOUTH

- Colleges and high schools should incorporate a component on workplace harassment in their school-based anti-bullying and anti-sexual assault efforts.

CHECKLIST ONE: LEADERSHIP AND ACCOUNTABILITY

The first step for creating a holistic harassment prevention program is for the leadership of an organization to establish a culture of respect in which harassment is not tolerated. Check the box if the leadership of your organization has taken the following steps

☐ Leadership has allocated sufficient *resources* for a harassment prevention effort

☐ Leadership has allocated sufficient *staff time* for a harassment prevention effort

☐ Leadership has *assessed* harassment *risk factors* and has taken steps to *minimize* those risks

Based on the commitment of leadership, check the box if your organization has the following components in place

☐ A harassment prevention *policy* that is *easy-to-understand* and that is *regularly communicated* to all employees

☐ A harassment reporting *system* that employees *know about* and is *fully resourced* and which accepts reports of harassment experienced and harassment observed

☐ *Imposition of discipline* that is prompt, consistent, and proportionate to the severity of the harassment, if harassment is determined to have occurred

☐ *Accountability* for mid-level managers and front-line supervisors to prevent and/or respond to workplace harassment

☐ Regular *compliance trainings for all employees* so they can recognize prohibited forms of conduct and know how to use the reporting system

☐ Regular *compliance trainings for mid-level managers and front-line supervisors* so they know how to prevent and/or respond to workplace harassment

Bonus points if you can check these boxes

☐ The organization conducts *climate surveys* on a regular basis to assess the extent to which harassment is experienced as a problem in the workplace

☐ The organization has implemented *metrics* for harassment response and prevention in supervisory employees' performance reviews

☐ The organization conducts *workplace civility training* and *bystander intervention training*

☐ The organization has *partnered with researchers* to evaluate the organization's holistic workplace harassment prevention effort

A reminder that this checklist is meant to be a useful tool in thinking about and taking steps to prevent harassment in the workplace, and responding to harassment when it occurs. It is not meant to convey legal advice or to set forth legal requirements relating to harassment. Checking all of the boxes does not necessarily mean an employer is in legal compliance; conversely, the failure to check any particular box does not mean an employer is not in compliance. REPORT OF THE CO-CHAIRS OF THE EEOC SELECT TASK FORCE ON THE STUDY OF HARASSMENT IN THE WORKPLACE

CHECKLIST TWO: AN ANTI-HARASSMENT POLICY

An anti-harassment policy is a key component of a holistic harassment prevention effort. Check the box below if your anti-harassment policy contains the following elements

☐ An unequivocal statement that harassment based on *any* protected characteristic will not be tolerated

☐ An easy-to-understand description of prohibited conduct, including examples

☐ A description of a reporting system – available to employees who experience harassment as well as those who observe harassment – that provides multiple avenues to report, in a manner easily accessible to employees

☐ A statement that the reporting system will provide a prompt, thorough, and impartial investigation

☐ A statement that the identity of an individual who submits a report, a witness who provides information regarding a report, and the target of the complaint, will be kept confidential to the extent possible consistent with a thorough and impartial investigation

☐ A statement that any information gathered as part of an investigation will be kept confidential to the extent possible consistent with a thorough and impartial investigation

☐ An assurance that the employer will take immediate and proportionate corrective action if it determines that harassment has occurred

☐ An assurance that an individual who submits a report (either of harassment experienced or observed) or a witness who provides information regarding a report will be protected from retaliation from co-workers and supervisors

☐ A statement that any employee who retaliates against any individual who submits a report or provides information regarding a report will be disciplined appropriately

☐ Is written in clear, simple words, in all languages commonly used by members of the workforce

A reminder that this checklist is meant to be a useful tool in thinking about and taking steps to prevent harassment in the workplace, and responding to harassment when it occurs. It is not meant to convey legal advice or to set forth legal requirements relating to harassment. Checking all of the boxes does not necessarily mean an employer is in legal compliance; conversely, the failure to check any particular box does not mean an employer is not in compliance. REPORT OF THE CO-CHAIRS OF THE EEOC SELECT TASK FORCE ON THE STUDY OF HARASSMENT IN THE WORKPLACE

CHECKLIST THREE: A HARASSMENT REPORTING SYSTEM AND INVESTIGATIONS

A reporting system that allows employees to file a report of harassment they have experienced or observed, and a process for undertaking investigations, are essential components of a holistic harassment prevention effort. Check the box below if your anti-harassment effort contains the following elements:

- [ ] A fully-resourced reporting process that allows the organization to respond promptly and thoroughly to reports of harassment that have been experienced or observed

- [ ] Employer representatives who take reports seriously

- [ ] A supportive environment where individuals feel safe to report harassing behavior to management

- [ ] Well-trained, objective, and neutral investigators

- [ ] Timely responses and investigations

- [ ] Investigators who document all steps taken from the point of first contact and who prepare a written report using guidelines to weigh credibility

- [ ] An investigation that protects the privacy of individuals who file complaints or reports, individuals who provide information during the investigation, and the person(s) alleged to have engaged in harassment, to the greatest extent possible

- [ ] Mechanisms to determine whether individuals who file reports or provide information during an investigation experience retribution, and authority to impose sanctions on those who engage in retaliation

☐ During the pendency of an investigation, systems to ensure individuals alleged to have engaged in harassment are not "presumed guilty" and are not "punished" unless and until a complete investigation determines that harassment has occurred

☐ A communication of the determination of the investigation to all parties and, where appropriate, a communication of the sanction imposed if harassment was found to have occurred

A reminder that this checklist is meant to be a useful tool in thinking about and taking steps to prevent harassment in the workplace, and responding to harassment when it occurs. It is not meant to convey legal advice or to set forth legal requirements relating to harassment. Checking all of the boxes does not necessarily mean an employer is in legal compliance; conversely, the failure to check any particular box does not mean an employer is not in compliance. REPORT OF THE CO-CHAIRS OF THE EEOC SELECT TASK FORCE ON THE STUDY OF HARASSMENT IN THE WORKPLACE

CHECKLIST FOUR: COMPLIANCE TRAINING

A holistic harassment prevention effort provides training to employees regarding an employer's policy, reporting systems and investigations. Check the box if your organization's compliance training is based on the following structural principles and includes the following content

Structural Principles

- ☐ Supported at the highest levels

- ☐ Repeated and reinforced on a regular basis

- ☐ Provided to all employees at every level of the organization

- ☐ Conducted by qualified, live, and interactive trainers

- ☐ If live training is not feasible, designed to include active engagement by participants

- ☐ Routinely evaluated and modified as necessary

Content of Compliance Training for All Employees

- ☐ Describes illegal harassment, and conduct that, if left unchecked, might rise to the level of illegal harassment

- ☐ Includes examples that are tailored to the specific workplace and the specific workforce

☐ Educates employees about their rights and responsibilities if they experience conduct that is not acceptable in the workplace

☐ Describes, in simple terms, the process for reporting harassment that is experienced or observed

☐ Explains the consequences of engaging in conduct unacceptable in the workplace

Content of Compliance Training for Managers and First-line Supervisors

☐ Provides easy-to-understand and realistic methods for dealing with harassment that they observe, that is reported to them, or of which they have knowledge or information, including description of sanctions for failing to use such methods

☐ Provides clear instructions on how to report harassing behavior up the chain of command, including description of sanctions for failing to report

☐ Encourages managers and supervisors to practice "situational awareness" and assess the workforces within their responsibility for risk factors of harassment

A reminder that this checklist is meant to be a useful tool in thinking about and taking steps to prevent harassment in the workplace, and responding to harassment when it occurs. It is not meant to convey legal advice or to set forth legal requirements relating to harassment. Checking all of the boxes does not necessarily mean an employer is in legal compliance; conversely, the failure to check any particular box does not mean an employer is not in compliance.

REPORT OF THE CO-CHAIRS OF THE EEOC SELECT TASK FORCE ON THE STUDY OF HARASSMENT IN THE WORKPLACE

Risk Factor	Risk Factor Indicia	Why This is a Risk Factor for Harassment	Risk Factor Specific Strategies to Reduce Harassment
Homogenous workforce	Historic lack of diversity in the workplace Currently only one minority in a work group (e.g., team, department, location)	Employees in the minority can feel isolated and may actually be, or at least appear to be, vulnerable to pressure from others. Employees in the majority might feel threatened by those they perceive as "different" or "other," or might simply be uncomfortable around others who are not like them	Increase diversity at all levels of the workforce, with particular attention to work groups with low diversity. Pay attention to relations among and within work groups.
Workplaces where some employees do not conform to workplace norms	"Rough and tumble" or single-sex-dominated workplace cultures Remarks, jokes, or banter that are crude, "raunchy," or demeaning	Employees may be viewed as weak or susceptible to abuse. Abusive remarks or humor may promote workplace norms that devalue certain types of individuals	Proactively and intentionally create a culture of civility and respect with the involvement of the highest levels of leadership. Pay attention to relations among and within work groups.

The strategies outlined in Part Three of this report (e.g., exercising leadership, holding people accountable for their actions, developing and enforcing effective policies and procedures, and conducting training) will help address all the risk factors listed in this chart. The strategies outlined in the last column of this chart are designed to address specific risk factors.

Risk Factor	Risk Factor Indicia	Why This is a Risk Factor for Harassment	Risk Factor Specific Strategies to Reduce Harassment
Cultural and language differences in the workplace	Arrival of new employees with different cultures or nationalities Segregation of employees with different cultures or nationalities	Different cultural backgrounds may make employees less aware of laws and workplace norms. Employees who do not speak English may not know their rights and may be more subject to exploitation. Language and linguistic characteristics can play a role in harassment.	Ensure that culturally diverse employees understand laws, workplace norms, and policies. Increase diversity in culturally segregated workforces. Pay attention to relations among and within work groups.
Coarsened Social Discourse Outside the Workplace	Increasingly heated discussion of current events occurring outside the workplace	Coarsened social discourse that is happening outside a workplace may make harassment inside the workplace more likely or perceived as more acceptable.	Proactively identity current events—national and local—that are likely to be discussed m the workplace. Remind the workforce of the types of conduct that are unacceptable in the workplace.

The strategies outlined in Part Three of this report (e.g., exercising leadership, holding people accountable for their actions, deseloping and enforcing effective policies and procedures, and conducting training) will help address all the risk factors listed in this chart. The strategies outlined in the last column of this chart are designed to address specific risk factors.

Risk Factor	Risk Factor Indicia	Why This is a Risk Factor for Harassment	Risk Factor Specific Strategies to Reduce Harassment
Young workforces	Significant number of teenage and young adult employees	Employees in their first or second jobs may be less aware of law's and workplace norms. Young employees may lack the self-confidence to resist unwelcome overtures or challenge conduct that makes them uncomfortable. Young employees may be more susceptible to being taken advantage of by coworkers or superiors, particularly those who may be older and more established in their positions. Young employees may be more likely to engage in harassment because they lack the maturity to understand or care about consequences.	Provide targeted outreach about harassment in high schools and colleges. Provide orientation to all new employees with emphasis on the employer's desire to hear about all complaints of unwelcome conduct. Provide training on how to be a good supervisor when youth are promoted to supervisory positions.

The strategies outlined in Part Three of this report (e.g., exercising leadership, holding people accountable for their actions, deseloping and enforcing effective policies and procedures, and conducting training) will help address all the risk factors listed in this chart. The strategies outlined in the last column of this chart are designed to address specific risk factors.

Risk Factor	Risk Factor Indicia	Why This is a Risk Factor for Harassment	Risk Factor Specific Strategies to Reduce Harassment
Workplaces with "high value" employees	Executives or senior managers Employees with high value (actual or perceived) to the employer, e.g. the "rainmaking" partner or the prized, grant-winning researcher	Management is often reluctant to jeopardize high value employee's economic value to the employer. High value employees may perceive themselves as exempt from workplace rules or immune from consequences of their misconduct.	Apply workplace rules uniformly, regardless of rank or value to the employer If a high-value employee is discharged for misconduct, consider publicizing that fact (unless there is a good reason not to).
Workplaces with significant power disparities	Low-ranking employees in organizational hierarchy Employees holding positions usually subject to the direction of others, e.g., administrative support staff, nurses, janitors, etc. Gendered power disparities (e.g., most of the low-ranking employees are female)	Supervisors feel emboldened to exploit low-ranking employees Low-ranking employees are less likely to understand complaint channels (language or education/training insufficiencies). Undocumented workers may be especially vulnerable to exploitation or the fear of retaliation.	Apply workplace rules uniformly, regardless of rank or value to the employer Pay attention to relations among and within work groups with significant power disparities.

The strategies outlined in Part Three of this report (e.g., exercising leadership, holding people accountable for their actions, developing and enforcing effective policies and procedures, and conducting training) will help address all the risk factors listed in this chart. The strategies outlined in the last column of this chart are designed to address specific risk factors.

Risk Factor	Risk Factor Indicia	Why This is a Risk Factor for Harassment	Risk Factor Specific Strategies to Reduce Harassment
Workplaces that rely on customer service or client satisfaction	Compensation directly tied to customer satisfaction or client service	Fear of losing a sale or tip may compel employees to tolerate inappropriate or harassing behavior.	Be wary of a "customer is always right" mentality in terms of application to unwelcome conduct.
Workplaces where work is monotonous or tasks are Low - intensity'	Employees are not actively engaged or "have time on their hands" Repetitive work	Harassing behavior may become a way to vent frustration or avoid boredom	Consider varying or restructuring job duties or workload to reduce monotony or boredom. Pay attention to relations among and within work groups with monotonous or low-intensity tasks
Isolated workplaces	Physically isolated workplaces Employees work alone or have few opportunities to interact with others	Harassers have easy access to their targets. There are no witnesses.	Consider restructuring work environments and schedules to eliminate isolated conditions. Ensure that workers in isolated work environments understand complaint procedures. Create opportunities for isolated workers to connect with each other (e.g., in person, on line) to share concerns.

The strategies outlined in Part Three of this report (e.g., exercising leadership, holding people accountable for their actions, deseloping and enforcing effective policies and procedures, and conducting training) will help address all the risk factors listed in this chart. The strategies outlined in the last column of this chart are designed to address specific risk factors.

SOURCES

The numbers in the paragraph above refer to where information was sited from in the study.

Documentation came from: Feldblum, Chai and Lipnic, Victoria. Select Task Force on the Study of Harassment in the Workplace: Executive Summary and Recommendations. June, 2016.

CHAPTER 10

LESSONS LEARNED FROM MY EXPERIENCE

"We should not judge people by their peak of excellence; but by the distance they have traveled from the point where they started."

—Henry Ward Beecher

1 I took the road less traveled.

    a I spoke up on a true issue and knew there was some risk for speaking the truth.

    b I knew what was right and what was wrong. I believed the right thing would be done.

    c In the past, truth had always overridden evil. In this case it didn't and I paid dearly for almost 10 years trying to recover from this experience.

    d Recovery was long for me. Yet you can learn from my mistakes and reduce the time of learning from my experience.

    e Per the EEOC Select Task Force on the Study of Harassment in the Work p20-p21:

ii "It begins with the reality that harassment causes personal harm to the victim.

iii Numerous studies have identified the damaging effects of mistreatment in the workplace, mainly focusing on sexual harassment.

iv Employees experiencing sexual harassment are more likely to suffer symptoms of depression, general stress and anxiety, posttraumatic stress disorder (PTSD) and overall impaired psychological well-being.

v The damaging personal effects of harassment are not limited to the victim.

vi There is a growing understanding that employees who observe or perceive mistreatment in their workplace can also suffer mental and physical harm.

vii One study found that employees, female and male alike, who observed hostility directed toward female coworkers (both incivility and sexually harassing behavior) were more likely to experience lower psychological well-being. These declines in mental health were, in turn, linked to lower physical well-being.

viii According to the study, the drivers of these effects can stem from empathy and worry for the victim, concern about the lack of fairness in the workplace or fear of becoming the next victim.

ix Whatever the case, if there is harassment in the workplace, more people than just the victim can be harmed."

2   I have learned that no journey is a straight line. Sometimes we move backwards, falter, get stuck, take a detour –yet in the end, as long as you remain committed to your truth, the journey will be one of a few tears, peace, love, and knowledge about life.

   a   Forgiveness for me was my first step on my path. I realized now why people become bitter and angry verses choosing happiness and enjoying life.

      i   If you do not forgive the only one hurt is you. It allowed me to eliminate revenge and allowed me some peace.

   b   Don't stand still because of fear or an experience.

   c   Take the risk to move forward and learn new skills or be open to new opportunities.

   d   Your plan may be changed but you can still be successful.

3   Realize that Human Resource (HR) and Employment Relations lawyers are there to represent the company – not you.

   a   In good corporate cultures, the company and HR may address the issues.

4   Understand the culture of the organization.

   a   Determine if the organization listens to employee concerns.

   b   If not, ask for a package right away.

   c   If they do not give you a package or resolve the situation, leave as quickly as you can.

   d   Avoid retaliation, as it impacts you as a person, as well as your family.

   e   People in the organization understand that something is not right

f Impacts the organization as people see something is not right, not good and question what is occurring. Actions are being taken that do not make sense.

    i I believe people learn to not speak up on issues based on what they have seen done to others. Culture allows this to happen.

5 Retaliation

If you are currently being retaliated against, the management will try to break you psychologically, ostracize you, and keep you from talking with others

a Seek whatever help you need.

b Talk to a counselor to work through issues.

c Take vacations so you can be prepared for the next retaliation.

d Consider meditation and a 10-day silent retreat to let it all go when you are through with the process.

e Seek professionals, family and friends that can support you.

6 Hire a lawyer to represent you, and understand what is involved in a case.

a Before you leave, ask your lawyer what can be done and your chances of winning.

b Determine if you want to move forward with the case.

c Understand what this process will be like.

d My lawyers had stated do not sign anything. Any time my boss, HR, employment lawyer tried to pressure me to sign something, my response was I cannot sign and will review with my lawyers.

7 Get away for time on your own, to process what happened to you.

    a I wrote in a journal throughout the process what was occurring to me at the company and by who, all details. Also, I had to type minutes from every meeting for the lawyers.

    b Keep copies of the emails that go back and forth.

    c What I have learned from my ten years of recovery is write your story right away and really get that detail down so you can really digest what happened and move forward.

    d I would never have remembered all of the details without this documentation.

    e A part of you will want to file the details in your mind as it is so hurtful. Don't allow yourself to suffer for years. Instead write until you have captured your whole story, write a book to help others, burn it, share it, decide what is beneficial for you to do based on who you are.

        i Going back into the pain when writing this story and releasing a lot of tears was key to me fully recovering.

        ii I have always been authentic. The trauma expert shared you cannot be fully authentic until you have integrated the situation you suffered from fully into your life. Now it is a part of who I am.

    f I had pain in my heart for three years after this experience.

        i 10 Day Silence Retreat: The only way I could recover from a pain in my heart was in 2013. I took a 10 day silent retreat. I learned "it is what it is" and accepted it. My pain in my heart went away.

g I used a variety of therapies including silence retreats, counselor's, pastor's, trauma expert, energy experts, and reiki experts to help me.

    i I did not understand why it took so much time to recover until I met the trauma expert. (see Chapter 6)

    ii Seek the help you need to relieve the pain, get over the experience and then use the lessons learned to help others.

    iii Share your story. Perpetrators will want you to keep you in silence. They can continue repeating the same action.

8 Write your story and review what happened.

    a Tell people what happened and then release it from your body and memory.

    b Capture all details right away as, over time, you can forget key points

    c Document, document and document.

        i This was key for me to write this story and document details for the lawyers.

        ii My project management skills allowed me to address in meetings who was assigned tasks or take away. Later I could point to that documentation when management tried to make issues mine.

    d If something feels wrong, it probably is. Listen to your gut instinct.

9 Get back in the workplace as quickly as you can.

    a Do not allow lack of trust to stop you from going to another company.

b   Ask questions of others who work at the company what their culture and organization is like.

c   Utilize your gut instinct when reviewing a new company and culture.

d   Utilize social media such as Glassdoor and other sources where company employees provide feedback.

e   Feel comfortable and be able to take the step forward.

f   If it's not the right decision, then look for something else.

g   Better to get back to work. Don't let others who may hurt your reputation stop you!

h   I was blessed with learning about my skill sets from others expertise and them sharing how my skills could be used.

i   I tried new roles that I would never have done if not for this circumstance.

10 We need a website to start capturing details about companies or social media

a   Make it be known the number of NDA's being signed at companies and Dollars associated with the NDA.

  i   An NDA is a legally binding contract that requires parties to keep confidentiality for a defined period of time. It's up to the parties to decide what would be considered confidential and what is not.

  ii   Understand which companies are demanding people agree to arbitration per their website or employee agreement.

b   Track the names of people who cause issues.

c Determine a way to validate action is true (less than 2% are false).

d Generally, I have to believe no one would go through this for money. The pain you must deal with is so great *no money* would be worth it.

We need to be concerned about companies that are now having people sign up on their websites or in employee contracts to internal negotiations(arbitration) if issues within the company. This is a direct cover up of issues needing resolution and beneficial for the company.

UNUSUAL THINGS THAT OCCURRED AT COMPANY

11 I leave my book with my written notes from meetings on my desk. I did this always but one day early in the process, my book is gone and no one returns it to me. I shared it was missing but it was never returned.

12 Adam's administrative assistant is fired shortly after I am addressing issues.

a She was very informed and could see what was occurring.

b She had access to all Adam's emails and his calendar.

13 Contractor lawyer at the company who I had been friends with stated she would be happy to represent me and would keep everything I shared with her confidential.

a She told me she had no commitment to company as a contractor beyond the contracts.

b She was the only one I trusted at the company. I should not have trusted her.

c   She called me the night I met with the lawyers first day to see what the % was the lawyers had stated of winning. I shared this with her as I was honest and thought she was my friend.

d   If she shared with the legal counsel her integrity and commitment to being lawyer would be at risk based on her verbal contract.

e   In the end, I believe company used her to get information.

14   I had a person that I had worked with at a previous company together who was working in HR at this company. I did not trust her going forward.

a   One time she met me at a restaurant and placed a satchel in the middle of the table. I thought she might be recording me but legally in Illinois she would need to have permission. It did not leave me trusting her going forward.

b   I let her know in December 2008 that if I brought a lawsuit against the company would she need to represent the company.

c   Not a smart move to have reached out to her way before we filed anything.

d   I actually thought this woman would work to do the right thing.

e   She represented the company line.

15   My computer seemed to have problems where my whole computer went down and needed to be taken by IT for about 2 days.

a   Do you think they duplicated what was on my computer during that time?

b   The company will do what they need to do.

16 Strange Meeting with a Friend

    a I have been friends with this employee since we started at the company same time and went through training together. (Understood over time he had a drinking problem.)

    b We met for lunch every once in a while, to share about our career experience at the company.

    c I found it interesting how I meet with this guy for lunch one day towards the end of my time at the company and had not seen him for quite some time. He orders wine and he says to me, "I did not know how you felt about me." My response was what are you talking about?

    d I am completely surprised by this comment and felt like I was being set up by the company. I looked around to see if we were being filmed or watched by company personnel. I did not share much information as something was not right.

    e Plus, when I am let go from the company, he tries to call me the next day.

        i He said I heard you are no longer with the company, call me.

    f Weird scenario. Let it go and stayed away from staying connected to him.

17 My mentor, Senior Vice President, who was assigned to me by the company for high performance mentor program.

    a He was an advocate for telling me I needed to get to personnel about my boss.

        ii He did not understand how a top performing employee would have a manager wanting to manage me so closely and had time to manage personal printing at his level.

b He put me in touch with the Head of the Mentor Program because my bosses' boss was Executive VP and Chief Administrative Officer for HR. Both of us knew that was a conflict of interest and lack of objectivity might not be there.

c Initially he discussed me coming to work within his organization.

d He had fallen off after about 6 months assumed someone talked with him about the case.

e He called me while I was on the train right after I was let go about 9 months after I had contact with him.

  i He seemed to be very informed that I was no longer there and wanted to see how I was doing.

  ii I was honest with him but realized later it was a set up by the company.

  iii What did they want to get from me that would benefit the company?

CHAPTER 11

CONSIDERATIONS FOR FORWARD THINKING COMPANIES AND INTEGRITY CULTURES

"The glue that holds all relationships together,
including the relationship between the leader and the led is trust,
and trust is based on integrity."

—BRIAN TRACY

ME TOO AND TIMES UP: ACCUSATIONS SHOULD MATTER TO BOARDS OF DIRECTORS (SOURCE IS FOLEY AND LARDNER PRESENTATION 2018)

LITIGATING AND SETTLING EXPENSES CAN COST MILLIONS

- Legal and investigation costs

- Settlements or judgments

- Impact on stock price and shareholders

- Impact on culture and people

REPUTATIONAL DAMAGE

- Applies to publicly traded companies, private companies, and non-profits
- Can and will impact recruitment/ retention of talented employees and employee productivity
- Abrupt termination/resignation of senior executives can lead to major organizational shifts and detract from organization's long term goals

BOARD HAS FIDUCIARY RESPONSIBILITY

- Board has a fiduciary responsibility to create a culture of compliance
- Company may need to disclose harassment claims to shareholders if the event involves senior executives or is pervasive within organization
  - Failure to adequately disclose sexual harassment settlements may prompt a federal investigation or private litigation

STATISTICS

- Approximately 28,000 charges of harassment annually over the last five years
- Guaranteed to go up in 2019
- 2016 Study – 85% of female employees reported experiencing workplace harassment

BOARD DUTIES AND ME TOO CLAIMS: EXAMPLE: FOX NEWS LAWSUIT

- Included claims against directors of 20th-Century Fox

- Alleged that directors breached fiduciary duties by failing to oversee compliance with and conduct a good faith investigation into known violators of laws and internal policies concerning sexual harassment and discrimination

- Factual allegations included:

  - Before hiring Roger Ailes, the board was aware of his "well-known reputation of being awful to women"

  - Board allows Ailes to "run Fox News as an independent fiefdom" that allowed a hostile work environment to grow and flourish

  - Board approved budgets for Fox News, which included amounts to fund the surveillance of employees

  - R. Murdoch's decision to give Ailes significant control over Fox News, and the board's complete failure to exercise independent oversight permitted a culture of rampant and obvious sexual harassment and exploitation to continue unabated for nearly 20 years

  - Result: $90,000,000 settlement

WHAT HAVE WE LEARNED FROM #METOO MOVEMENT?

- Companies and their boards should look for patterns of poor behavior from such signals as high turnover, low morale, a culture that evidences lack of respect and courtesy

- Organizational Culture Matters

- Tolerating rude and improper behavior makes people hesitant to speak up for bad or illegal behavior
- Some companies now task internal teams to perform cultural audits and report results directly to audit committees. (A company that is a leader will do this)

- Power—actual or perceived—matters

PROBLEMS CAN COME FROM OUTSIDE AN ORGANIZATION, NOT JUST FROM INTERNAL EMPLOYEES

- Examples include independent contractors
    - Weinstein Company, Fox held liable
- Vendors, and customers
    - Employees harassing them
    - E.g., law firm client hitting on law firm associate

WHAT BOARDS SHOULD BE ASKING MANAGEMENT

- How does the company currently handle sexual harassment claims?
    - When and how is the board informed about such complaints?
    - What is the "who", "what", "where", "when" and "how" with respect to the company's policies and procedures for reporting sexual harassment claims to the board?
- What is the company's diversity and inclusion training program?
    - Is it a check the box approach limited to an on-line module?

- Is it an organized, serious, thoughtful approach that permeates throughout the organization?

- How does one test via objective metrics?

- Survey employees regularly

- Surveys are a great tool to help isolated employees be heard

- Does the Board have access to information about prior complaints and outcomes, especially involving CEO and senior management?

- Is the Board notified immediately if an accusation is made against the CEO or a member of senior management team?

  - Boards should consider whether to require board approval of any settlements, especially if they involve C-Suite or senior managers

BOARD'S RESPONSE TO A #METOO COMPLAINT

- Complaint Against CEO? Or Senior Management?

  - If again the CEO or other officers, Board must be notified about-if not lead-the process

  - Notified about senior management and Board is notified and has appropriate oversight

  - Other complaints, the process should be led by management, yet reported to the board

  - Timing of response is key-address with legal team and internal investigation team

- Range of Responses
    - Nothing, review and unpublicized discipline taken, paid administrative leave, unpaid administrative leave, termination without cause, termination with cause, claw back salary, bonuses and stock

OTHER PRACTICAL CONSIDERATIONS

- Review employment contracts with current and future senior management
    - Review "for clause" provisions closely-do they include violation of anti-harassment policies?
    - Consider "morals clause"
    - Consider strengthening clawback and indemnification provisions: should the executive the executive be required to indemnify company if claims are proven?
    - Consider inclusion of restrictions on shareholders voting rights
- Review employment practices liability insurance
- M&A Implications for buyer's due diligence review: add to review of sexual harassment complaints against management to checklist

HOW THE BOARDS CAN MITIGATE FUTURE RISKS (UTILIZE HUMAN RESOURCES)

- Work with management to adopt a 21st-century anti-harassment policy
- Ensure anti-harassment policies extend to the use of the company's technology

- The company should have the right, but not the obligation, to review and access any messages or information transmitted on company systems

- Discuss additional internal reporting mechanisms, such as an anonymous hotline or ombudsman

  - Hotline or more protected, concerted activity (to combat disadvantage of "first reporters" who face credibility hurdle and are more likely to be retaliated against)

- Address diversity issues at the board/management level

  - Companies with strong female leadership tend to have fewer governance-related controversies

  - Equal representation in executive and director positions is one of the best ways to promote a business culture in which all employees feel safe and valued

- More questions about the power and pay differential

- More emphasis on unconscious /subconscious biases

JUDY FOLEY'S SUGGESTION ON MEASUREMENTS OF SUCCESS FOR HARASSMENT AND ANY SEXUAL MISCONDUCT

- Number of NDAs and arbitration agreements annually, last five years money paid out for cover-up, and legal expenses

  - If the details of the NDAs and arbitration agreements came out, how would this impact your company?

- Track total number of issues by people within organization

- How many people have addressed issues?

- Need to eliminate paragraphs in employment contracts about negotiations internally within the company with sex discrimination, harassment, and retaliation. This only hides the problem, eliminates law suits and key question is root cause resolved.

QUESTIONS TO ASK ABOUT YOUR CULTURE

- What is the cost of keeping the executive and the message it sends within the organization?

    - If you want the best people, why not uphold a culture that does not tolerate unacceptable behavior? Be consistent in your approach and all win.

    - What is the cost of reporting other issues within the organization when others see how this is handled?

    - What is the reputational impact for the victim and person addressing the issue?

    - What is the cost for victims and their families?

- People understand when issues are occurring to some extent

- Retaliation in the workplace

    - What message does retaliation for speaking the truth send to others in the organization?

SOURCE

Foley & Lardner, National Directors Institute Executive Exchange. Me Too Meets the Boardroom Presentation. October 25, 2018.

CHAPTER 12

CALL TO ACTION

"To those who abuse: the sin is yours, the crime is yours, and the shame is yours. To those who protect the perpetrators: blaming the victims only masks the evil within, making you as guilty as those who abuse. Stand up for the innocent or go down with the rest."

—Flora Jessop, Church of Lies

The #MeToo Movement has cast a new light on the issue of sexual harassment and sexual assault, while Times Up has highlighted sexual assault, harassment and inequality in the workplace and social media has become a mainstream tool that has successfully high-lighted a number of sexual misconduct issues to be openly discussed and addressed. These issues cannot be discarded by companies as they have done in the past. They will no longer go away and it remains the responsibility of each company to create and sustain a culture not based upon the preferences of a few, but the inclusion of all to support and ever increasing diversity in our workforce. This is no longer a secondary issue to be considered, but rather a primary objective of corporations and businesses who desire to hire the best and brightest into their organization. With the advent of social media such as Facebook, LinkedIn, Glassdoor and other venues, employees can now quickly assess the environment and culture that exists within an organization before considering a firm. No longer are the practices of a firm quietly discussed –if you now want to hire those that can make a difference in your company it is critical that you provide an environment that creates a difference and meaning-ful work for them. Without it, you remain a victim of your own practices and will suffer many of the consequences discussed earlier.

For women or men in America who have historically come for-ward with stories of harassment, abuse, and sexual assault, there has not been a level playing field. But with stories now publicly shared and a growing sense for the need of equality and proper treatment in the workplace, the opportunity to create change is now more possible than ever before due to the courageous actions of a few who have brought this issue front and center to boardrooms, schools, hospitals, churches and politics. However, sustaining the conversation and maintaining its relevance is incumbent on all of us in whatever role we play with our society. Each of us is a leader of someone –whether a child, associates at work, or the head of a large corporation leading thousands of employees. And this change must continue to occur and be nurtured at each level of society if we are to be ultimately measured on our success in changing the status quo. This can no longer be the #metoo movement but rather the #wetoo movement. All of us need to actively engage in the day to day struggles that come with this type of change. Without helping each other on this path we risk backsliding towards uncertainty and an environment where this behavior remains unchecked. This book is a culmination of ten years of on-going recovery that will forever leave an indelible mark on my life. And while I've found my place of peace and am moving forward, the final question to all of us is how many like me remain in the shadows and are walking wounded never to openly discuss what has transpired in their life or others that may have committed suicide based on losing hope? We'll never know, but our ability to help prevent this from continuing is the ultimate objective of this book. Sharing creates more sharing and open conversation, and with support from each of us at all levels of society we can change the future. It's now time the #metoo movement becomes the #wetoo movement, and we collectively support not only those who are currently suffering, but those who are making a difference and changing the rules that have governed these practices. In the end, it does take a village to make a difference. I hope you join me in moving this village forward…#wetoo.